This Book Belongs To:
George Plunkett
940-382-7572

MW00450448

The Amazing Tale of Mr. Herbert and His Fabulous Alpine Cowboys Baseball Club

Denton Senior Center
509 Bell Avenue
Denton, TX 76201

West Texas Field of Dreams

A crowd gathers on game day at "Fabulous Kokernot Field." The ballpark, complete with its own Texas oil well, was built by Herbert L. Kokernot Jr. in 1947 for his beloved Alpine Cowboys semipro baseball club. Kokernot, a multimillionaire cattle rancher and financier, built the park on a piece of his ranch land on the outskirts of the far West Texas town of Alpine. The small college town of 6,800 people, located in the heart of the Big Bend region, lies four hours southeast of El Paso and three hours from a major airport. It's a place where distance is measured in time, not miles. Surrounded by mountains and situated at a "fly-ball carrying" elevation of 4,400 feet, Kokernot Field would have been a hitter's dream if not for its Texas-sized proportions. At 340 feet down each line, 370 feet in the alleys, and 430 feet to the centerfield wall, which rises another ten feet in height above the ten-foot fence, the park's dimensions rival those of many major league fields. The first-class baseball stadium became known as the "Best Little Ballpark in the World."

His Brand

Mr. Herbert, as Herbert Kokernot was known, lines up outside the right-field wall of Kokernot Field with the 1958 edition of the Alpine Cowboys. The light poles of his state-of-the-art lighting system can be seen behind him. The wall of the ballpark, made of a distinctive native red stone, proudly displays the cattle brand of Kokernot's famous O6 Ranch. The O6 is the oldest recorded brand in the Big Bend region. At one time, the brand was carried by 35,000 head of cattle on 400,000 acres of Kokernot land. The O6 brand was displayed liberally throughout the ballpark and emblazoned on the Cowboys' uniforms. Over the years Mr. Herbert would employ his players at the O6 Ranch in order to assist them with their college tuitions. "The main reason I sponsor this ball club is because of those college boys. I like 'em, and I like to help them," he said. Front row, left to right: Joe Horlen, Bill Horlen, Roy Lewis, Ray Van Cleef, Mike Ellis (batboy), Bobby Quinn, Gary Herrington, Ron Bennett, and Toby Newton. Back row, left to right: Gene Leek, Bert Lattimore, Jerry Wolff, Chuck Ellis (coach), Herbert Kokernot Jr. (sponsor), Tom Chandler (manager), Roy Peterson, Mickey Sullivan, Tommy Snow, and George Martin. Absent: Tommy Shields, Freddy Davis, Joe Curtin, Bud Osborne, and Tommy Cronin.

The Amazing Tale of Mr. Herbert and His Fabulous

ALPINE

Cowboys

BASEBALL CLUB

An Illustrated History of the Best Little Semipro Baseball Team in Texas

by DJ Stout, with an Introduction by Nicholas Dawidoff

Denton Senior Center
509 Bell Avenue
Denton, TX 76201

UNIVERSITY OF TEXAS PRESS ❧ AUSTIN, TEXAS

Clifton and Shirley Caldwell Texas Heritage Series

Publication of this work was made possible in part by support from Clifton and Shirley Caldwell and a challenge grant from the National Endowment for the Humanities.

Copyright © 2010 by University of Texas Press
Text copyright © 1989 by Nicholas Dawidoff
Text copyright © 2010 by DJ Stout
All rights reserved
Printed in China
First Edition, 2010

For reasons of economy and speed, this volume has been printed from camera-ready copy furnished by the author, who assumes full responsibility for its contents.

Photographs from the Hunter and Casey collections are published with permission from the Archives of the Big Bend at the Bryan Wildenthal Memorial Library at Sul Ross State University.

Requests for permission to reproduce material from this work should be sent to:

Permissions
University of Texas Press
P.O. Box 7819, Austin, TX 78713-7819
www.utexas.edu/utpress/about/permission.html

♾ The paper used in this book meets the minimum requirements of ANSI/NISO Z39.48-1992 (R1997) (Permanence of Paper).

Library of Congress Cataloging-in-Publication Data

Stout, DJ
The amazing tale of Mr. Herbert and his fabulous Alpine Cowboys baseball club : an illustrated history of the best little semipro baseball team in Texas / by DJ Stout ; with an Introduction by Nicholas Dawidoff. — 1st ed.
    p. cm. — (Clifton and Shirley Caldwell Texas heritage series)
ISBN 978-0-292-72334-4 (cloth : alk. paper)
1. Alpine Cowboys (Baseball team) — History. 2. Minor league baseball — Texas — Alpine — History. 3. Baseball — Texas — Alpine — History. 4. Kokernot, Herbert L. 5. Baseball team owners — Texas — Biography. I. Title.

GV875.A565S86 2010
796.357'6309764932—dc22

2010018876

Introduction first published as "The Best Little Ballpark in Texas (or Anywhere Else)" in *Sports Illustrated*, July 31, 1989. Reprinted with permission from Nicholas Dawidoff in its original form.

Cover: Alpine Cowboys team, 1951, by Charles Hunter.
Page 9: Infielder Bobby Frey, 1955, at Kokernot Field, by Charles Hunter.
Page 12: Herbert Kokernot Jr., by Charles Hunter.

Book and jacket design by DJ Stout and Christen Collier Pentagram Design, Austin, Texas.

To the pitcher, Doyle E. Stout Sr.

Light Year

A night game viewed from the grandstands of Kokernot Field. In 1958, the year before the Cowboys joined the professional ranks of the Sophomore League, Kokernot added lights to his ballpark. That was one of the last major improvements Mr. Herbert made to Kokernot Field before the Cowboys signed on to become a farm team for the big league Red Sox, and he spared no expense to get the best lights available at the time. The $75,000 lighting system consisted of 272 1,500-watt globes placed on 90-foot steel towers. When the lights were turned on at the opening game of the 1958 season, they were comparable to, if not better than, those of any major league ballpark in the country.

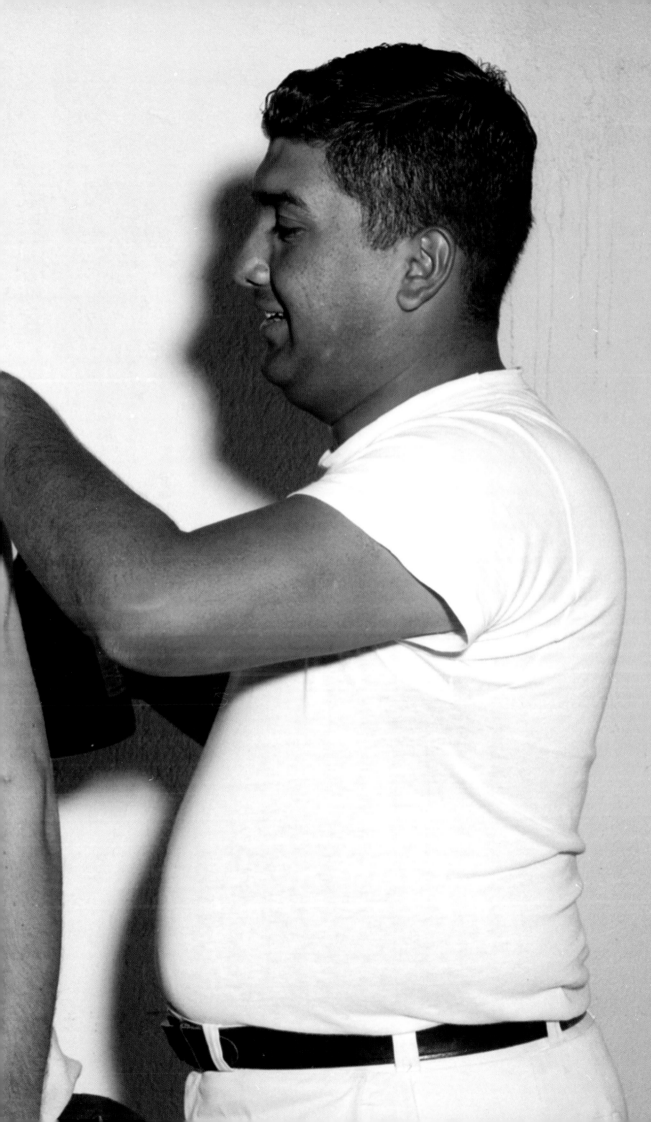

Growing Pains

In 1958 semipro baseball finally struck out. The Korean War had ended, and the U.S. military, which had been a major source of top-notch baseball competition for the Alpine Cowboys over the years, wasn't fielding teams anymore. And oil companies, which had been the other major provider of semipro clubs, had hit hard economic times and weren't sponsoring baseball teams as frequently either. The Cowboys had been running up high scores against their existing competition for the past several years and it had become increasingly difficult to find worthy opponents. So when the Boston Red Sox organization approached Mr. Herbert and made the pitch to base its Class D Sophomore League team at Kokernot Field, he told them that he would do it as long as they kept the name Cowboys. The Red Sox agreed, and so on opening day in 1959 the new professional version of the Cowboys made its debut with the ridiculously wordy name Alpine–Davis Mountains Cowboys. The all-inclusive name was an attempt to snag a wider audience in the region, but it was quickly dropped and ultimately forgotten by Alpine fans. It was a sign of things to come for the fledgling pro team. Pictured: Cowboys trainer Manny Benavides works on Don Pressley's sore pitching muscles in 1959.

My Father's Left Arm

BY DJ STOUT

Father's Day

The first time my 18-year-old dad (opposite page) opened up his locker under the grand-stands of Kokernot Field in 1952 and saw his two crisp pinstriped uniforms, a soft leather glove, and a shiny new pair of cleats, he broke down in tears. Growing up and playing sandlot ball in the Oak Cliff neighborhood of Dallas, he had never been able to afford decent baseball equipment. Now he was sitting in a luxurious spacious locker room in a spectacular baseball park in a strange and wonderful place he had never heard of. His lodging and all of his meals were provided, his tuition at Sul Ross College was paid, and the best thing of all was that he could play baseball, his first love, every single day. He must have felt like he had died and gone to a West Texas heaven.

Last summer I thought I saw a ghost in Alpine, Texas. I was sitting in the grandstands of the recently spruced-up Kokernot Field watching a ball game between the South Louisiana Pipeliners and the newly reinstated Big Bend Cowboys. Until that summer of 2009 it had been nearly fifty years since professional baseball had been played in Alpine. The story of how my father played for the legendary Alpine Cowboys, and the team's wealthy owner and rancher, Herbert Kokernot Jr., has always been a major part of my family's history and lore, but this was the first time I had ever witnessed an actual game at the storied Kokernot Field. It was a beautiful summer night. A dry cool breeze blowing off the distant mountains made the ballpark remarkably comfortable for a late July evening in the West Texas desert. It was almost chilly. Many of the spectators sat with their arms tightly folded around themselves, trying to fend off the cool night air. An elderly lady sitting next to me sent her grandson to the parking lot to fetch a sweater out of her pickup truck. And that's when I saw her.

At the end of an inning the Big Bend Cowboys took the field again, and as the lanky Cowboys pitcher trotted out to the mound, a petite young woman sitting a few rows over stood up and gazed silently out at the emerald and orange playing field, resplendent in the stadium lights. Her dark hair was tied up in a scarf, and she wore a crisp white shirt and straight-legged jeans tucked into tall western boots. A soft light from the ballpark fell on her, and she glowed. She stood rigid and

completely still for the longest time, her eyes never diverting from the direction of the pitcher's mound. Her glow became an aura, and I could not take my eyes off of this mysterious woman. Something about her scarf and starched white shirt made me think of a simpler, more innocent time. Then it hit me. I was looking at an apparition, a vision from the past. I imagined my beautiful 17-year-old mother, Elizabeth Armstrong, at an Alpine Cowboys game in 1954. She was standing up in the stands to get a good look at my handsome athletic father, striding confidently out to the mound to begin the inning. He was a charming left-handed pitcher from Dallas named Doyle Stout, whom she had just met at a Sul Ross College social, and she was intrigued. My young mother might have stood in that exact spot in those very same grandstands of the fabulous Kokernot Field. At that moment, I'm sure that my mother, an identical twin from the tiny town of Van Horn, only two hours north of Alpine, never dreamed that she would be married to that worldly southpaw pitching star from the big city and that she would soon give birth to her first son, Doyle Stout Jr. (DJ), in a little hospital just a long home run from the center-field wall of Kokernot Field.

I have always said that I am the son of two cowboys. A cow-punching West Texas cowboy, my grandfather Pat Armstrong, and a baseball-playing Alpine Cowboy, my dad.

My mother's father, Pat Armstrong, worked as a cowhand when he was a young man, and then he was

the foreman of a ranch outside of Toyah, located between Pecos and Kent, in a dry and desolate part of West Texas. His real name was Hervey Raymond Armstrong, but everyone called him Pat, which had been the name of one of his family's favorite mules when he was a kid. My grandmother Jane happened to get her first teaching job in Toyah after she had completed only two years of

Two Cowboys

My parents on a date at Big Bend National Park around the time they first met (right). My mother, Elizabeth Armstrong, was a freshman at Sul Ross College and had been introduced to my father, Doyle Stout, at a college social. My dad, who was from Dallas, had been playing baseball for the Alpine Cowboys and the Sul Ross Lobos and was a sportswriter for the college. My mother and her twin sister, Lora, who was also attending Sul Ross, were from the small town of Van Horn, Texas, about two hours north of Alpine, and had rarely traveled far from home. My mother's father, Pat Armstrong, pictured with his niece (opposite page), was a foreman at a ranch in Toyah, Texas, when my grandmother, Jane, first met him. Jane had been teaching school in Toyah and was smitten by the tall West Texas cowboy.

college at Wichita Falls Junior College. She was officially required to get two more years of college before she could get a permanent teaching certificate, but times were tough and teachers were needed in rural West Texas. She was only 18 years old when she went to Toyah to teach, and she was immediately assigned to the entire Mexican school. Originally from Gorman, in Central Texas, Jane had never actually seen a Mexican before. She loved teaching there, though, and she also coached the girls basketball team.

When Jane first got to town, she needed a place to live, so she moved into Pat Armstrong's brother's family home to room. They liked her a lot and thought she was quite a dish in her stylish flapper clothes and little spit curls, so they introduced her to Pat. Jane thought he was the most exciting cowboy she had ever seen, with his horses, fancy cowboy boots, and big ten-gallon hat. The pair wanted to get married, but Jane's family moved her away from Toyah to keep her from marrying the older West Texas cowboy. After a year the couple decided to get married anyway. When Pat came up to Gorman for the wedding, he had just been paid by the ranch so he had only large bills. The businesses in the small town of Gorman couldn't cash them, so Jane ended up paying for the whole wedding.

When they were first married, Jane and Pat lived on a ranch outside of Toyah. Pat worked on the ranch and was doing well, running some of his own cattle, but then right before their first son, John, was born the Depression hit. They had a hard time financially after that for many years. Pat had to do a variety of odd jobs to make ends meet, including one job where he was paid in script to build a long barbed-wire fence that stretched along the side of the road between Toyah and Pecos. I think that fence is still there today. My hardworking grandfather had big hands, like well-worn catcher's mitts, and he kind of sauntered like John Wayne when he walked. For the most part, he was a fairly quiet man, but like a lot of West Texas cowboys he was a wonderful storyteller. Texas storytelling is an art unto itself. The key to it is to tell an entertaining tale even if you have to exaggerate the facts a little bit.

One of my personal favorites was a story my Grandpa Armstrong told about driving cattle. As the story goes, he and a bunch of cowboys were moving a herd of cattle through some brushy country, and some of the cows kept wandering off into the scraggly bushes and thorny mesquite. That was making a lot of extra work for the cowboys, who would have to break away from the main herd to chase down renegade cows. One remedy was to take short branches from the mesquite, break them off to just the right length, and then jam them into the cows' eyes so that the sticks kept their eyelids propped wide open. A cow that was unable to close its eyes would hesitate to wander off into the brush and would stay with the herd in the open range. That was according to my grandfather, of course. As an editorial art director, book designer, and author for more than thirty years, I have often credited my grandfather's penchant for telling entertaining tall tales as an influence on my choice of career. I'm convinced that my strongly held belief—that effective writing, photography, and design is all about creating good narratives and telling an entertaining story—originally came from a hardworking West Texas cowboy named after a mule.

My dad's father, The Most Reverend Harold Stout Sr. of Dallas, Texas, lost his father at the age of three and his mother at the age of 12, which left him in charge of a family of four children at a very young age. He never finished high school, and he began to run with a rough crowd. Soon he developed a reputation as a wild and angry young man. When he was about 23 years old, my grandfather rode his Harley Davidson to New York City just for the hell of it, and on the trip he had a near-fatal accident. The motorcycle flipped over, and he was

pinned under the bike for more than 18 hours in freezing weather. After a long struggle, he managed to free himself from the wreckage, and then he caught a bus back to Dallas. The near-death experience alarmed my grandfather, so when he was invited by some friends to attend an evangelistic roadside tent revival, he went along. The revival changed him—he was born again.

As an enthusiastic convert to the Pentecostal religion my grandfather vigorously embraced all the fundamental tenets of the sect. He believed in speaking in tongues, hands-on healing, and tithing. In Harold's newfound orthodoxy, there was no drinking, no tobacco, no movies, and no jewelry. He quickly became a minister and developed a knack for fiery oratory. His "hellfire and brimstone" sermons would bring the wrath of God Almighty down on all who attended his services. Quite often my father and his mother, Ethel, would be the only ones in the audience. Harold became a fairly popular preacher among his Pentecostal brethren, and soon he had his own weekly radio show that was transmitted from the top of the Stoneleigh Hotel in downtown Dallas. On several of my family's trips to Dallas to visit my grandparents, my two brothers and I would go up to the radio station to sing religious songs on the program. My grandparents seemed to call everyone "brother" or "sister," and so for the longest time we just thought that they had a lot of siblings.

Grandpa Stout loved to sing in the church, and his favorite hymn was "When the Role Is Called Up Yonder." My dad could never figure out where "Yonder" was exactly, but he assumed that it was probably "Up There" somewhere. My grandfather also played the banjo, mandolin, and piano and was very disappointed that my father wasn't interested in playing instruments or in church music—or in the church at all, for that matter. My grandfather wanted my dad to attend church almost every night or at least three or four times a week. It was a frustrating lifestyle for a young athletic high school boy.

My father was good at sports, so at an early age he began to attract attention and be praised for his athletic abilities. Sports became his escape from a restrictive home life. He spent every minute of his spare time at the school yard, playing basketball, football, softball, and especially baseball. He even built his own pitching mound. Every day after school he would play baseball at the sandlot until it got dark or until his very physical father chased him home with a paddle.

My grandfather didn't support my dad's enthusiasm for baseball. He never once played catch with my father, he wouldn't drive him to practices, and he never

ever attended a game. He thought that baseball was a frivolous activity, "the devil's work," and a big waste of time. It was just a silly game that distracted his son from the important mission of the church. When my father first started playing organized baseball, he had to ride his bike ten miles to practice and then back home late at night, with no lights and through some sketchy neighborhoods.

My left-handed father became a good little pitcher, and when he was about 12 years old he was recruited by the Salvation Army baseball club. In order to play for the team he needed baseball cleats, a uniform, a hat, and a glove. His parents wouldn't pay for any of it. My grandfather didn't make a lot of money from his small driveway paving business to begin with, but the majority of his limited income went to the church anyway. A generous elderly man at the Salvation Army bought my dad the uniform and hat, and another man paid for his shoes. My grandfather was not impressed that my dad had made the team. He just wanted him to be home in time for church.

My father attended Crozier Tech High School in downtown Dallas, which was a long round-trip bus ride from his home in Oak Cliff. He initially went to the school because his older brother, Harold Jr., had been enrolled in a technical training program there. It turned out that Crozier Tech had an excellent baseball program with a great coach, and the team would often play Adamson High School, which was coached by Tom Chandler. My dad beat Adamson every time he pitched against them. Tom Chandler, who eventually became the manager of the Alpine Cowboys, took notice. In 1952, when my father was a senior, Crozier Tech made it to the Texas State Championship tournament, which was played at Disch Falk Field at The University of Texas at Austin. His ragtag "Cinderella Team," without proper uniforms, gloves, or equipment, had managed to win thirteen consecutive games and defied the odds to represent the entire greater Dallas-Fort Worth area in the State finals. In one of the semifinal games of the tournament, my father put on an impressive pitching performance, establishing the Texas State high school record of 21 strikeouts in nine innings and setting Crozier Tech up for the final championship game. After the exciting record-breaking semifinal game, my dad, who was scheduled to pitch in the championship game the next day, was so hyped up and full of nervous energy that he went for a long five-mile run instead of resting to build his strength back up. It was a youthful mistake. Crozier Tech ended up with second place in the State tournament, losing the final championship game

Team Tech
My dad's high school baseball team in Dallas, Crozier Tech (opposite), came in second place at the Texas State Championship finals in 1952. At a semifinal game during that tournament, my father set the Texas high school strikeout record and was invited by Cowboys manager Tom Chandler and owner Herbert Kokernot to play for their semipro team in Alpine, Texas. Crozier Tech's baseball coach, Charles Stubblefield (top row, left) was an inspirational coach and a mentor to the young squad. My father, Doyle Stout (top row, second from left), and R. L. Patterson (top row, right), both ended up playing for the Cowboys.

to Houston's Reagan High School, but my father was about to become one of the biggest winners of the tournament anyway.

After the championship game, Crozier Tech's coach, Charles Stubblefield, introduced my dad to Tom Chandler, the manager of the Alpine Cowboys, and to the team's owner, Herbert Kokernot. The two gentlemen asked my father what his plans were for the immediate future and whether he would be interested in playing baseball in a place called Alpine, Texas, for a semipro team called the Cowboys. My dad had never heard of Alpine, and he wasn't really sure where it was. He received no further details about salary or any other terms and conditions about joining the team, but he accepted the offer anyway.

My dad was only 18 years old, with no plans for college and no means to get there even if he had wanted to. He had just led his high school team to a respectable finish in the Texas State Championship finals, and he was still reeling from the excitement of setting the Texas high school strikeout record. He really hadn't thought

much about what would happen after that. His future was uncertain, but he knew that he did not want to return to his past. He had felt trapped by his strict religious home life. Baseball had been his escape hatch, and now the sport was opening a new door. He was about to begin a journey out west that would change his life forever. When my father left Dallas to play for the Alpine Cowboys and to attend Sul Ross College, he never looked back and he seldom went home. His parents did not understand what he was doing, and they really didn't seem that interested. My grandfather's dogmatism and his strict religious zealotry did not allow for anything else. In my father's family, there had been no room for temporal matters, no debates over world events, no high-minded discussions about divergent points of view—and absolutely no sports talk.

In Alpine Mr. Kokernot paid my dad's tuition and covered all his living expenses, and so my father went on to earn a master's degree in political science. While he was at Sul Ross, my dad became a sportswriter and publicist for the college. During that time he developed a lifelong love of writing and journalism, which he passed on to me. Later, when my dad became an officer in the Marine Corps, we moved practically every year.

I was always the new kid, so I began to produce little newspapers that I would hand out to the neighbors. My papers started out as mostly cartoons, but then the comic papers began to include more written content. My dad would help me write them (or mostly write them), and he would buy me rudimentary copying machines to print the newspapers.

When I was a bit older, I would start newspapers at the schools I attended, if they didn't have one already, or I would join the staffs of newspapers that were already in existence. In college I worked at the university newspaper, designing the ads and drawing comic strips that became quite popular with the student body. I loved being part of a newspaper or magazine staff. It was exciting being a part of the team that was breaking the news or pissing off the university's administration, and since I moved all the time, that team gave me a readily available group of friends and peers. So, like my dad, I developed a love of journalism and editorial design, which eventually led to my 13-year stint as the art director of *Texas Monthly* magazine and my 30-year career as a publication designer. The cross-country moves exposed my parents and their three young impressionable boys to different points of view and fresh ways of thinking. It opened our minds and made us tolerant of others. After the Marines, my dad became a successful businessman overseas. His college education had been invaluable to his career path, and baseball is what made it all possible. In a real sense my father's left arm paid for his education, which paved the way for his own amazing personal transformation.

The legend of the Alpine Cowboys has been a major part of my family's story for as long as I can remember. Like air and water, it's always been there. The tale of the West Texas rancher with the funny name ("Mr. Coconuts" was what my two brothers and I called him when we were little) has been such a staple of my heritage that he has evolved into a kind of distant relative, like a beloved grandparent or a favorite uncle.

Around 1961 or 1962, my father, who had joined the Marines after college, was stationed at the sprawling Camp Pendleton Marine Corps base in Southern California. We lived on base housing in an area called Wire Mountain. I remember clomping around the backyard in my dad's "Alpine Cowboys boots" that were so big on me they came up over my knees. The boots had been presented to my dad and his Alpine Cowboys teammates by Herbert Kokernot at the end of the 1952 season. It had been one of Mr. Herbert's yearly traditions. The pointy-toed red and white cowboy boots, custom-made by Tony Lama himself in El Paso, featured a pair of crossed baseball bats, the words "Alpine Cowboys," and the O6 brand.

One of my father's best friends from his days as an Alpine Cowboy was a right-handed pitcher named Ivan Abromowitz. Ivan had been in the minor leagues with the New York Yankees right after high school and then played for the Fort Bliss Falcons in El Paso while he was serving in the Army. At the end of the regular season in 1951, Ivan and three other Fort Bliss players, including Pete Swain, were picked up by the Alpine Cowboys to play in the National Baseball Congress semipro tournament in Wichita, Kansas. Ivan ended up moving to Alpine, where he attended Sul Ross College and became my dad's roommate during his junior and senior years. When we were living on base at Camp

Pendleton, and I was only about four years old, Ivan gave my father a German Shepherd named Jupiter. Our small house backed up to an open area, where military war games were frequently staged. Jupiter, a young energetic dog, would bark constantly and then jump over the fence to chase after the tanks and soldiers. That was a source of much frustration for my father, who kept nailing boards higher and higher up the fence to try to keep the dog from escaping.

One evening my dad came home from work, and I was missing. He walked frantically around the neighborhood, knocking on doors, but nobody had seen me. The military police and the fire department arrived, and the neighbors were running all over the place searching for me. My dad was beginning to panic, and then off in the distance he could hear a familiar bark. It sounded a lot like Jupiter, and he just couldn't believe his bad luck. Not only was his four-year-old son missing, but now the damn dog had jumped the fence again and was barking his fool head off. "Why now?" my dad wondered.

It was getting dark, but in the moonlight my father could just make out the form of Jupiter at the top

of a hill about 500 yards away. He was standing under a tall water tower, and when my dad called for him, he wouldn't come. He barked and barked and barked, so my father had to trudge up the hill to get him, but the dog would not budge. He stood rigid as a statue, barking and staring down at an open pipe, 12 to 14 inches in diameter, that was buried vertically into the ground. What a surprise it must have been when my dad peered

Good Shepherd
My father, my brother John, and I pose with our German Shepherd, Jupiter. The dog had been given to us by Ivan Abromowitz, a former Alpine Cowboys teammate and my dad's best friend. Ivan had a German Shepherd of his own named Tsar, who, as the story goes, introduced Ivan to his future wife, Rosemary. In 1962 my family lived in an area called Wire Mountain on the sprawling Marine Corps base at Camp Pendleton in Southern California. Jupiter started out as just a dog, but then he became "The Wonder Dog."

down into the pipe and saw my little face looking back at him from about a foot below the surface. Somehow I had managed to climb into the pipe and had gotten stuck, with one leg folded behind me and my hands wedged down at my side. I wasn't crying, but I was obviously scared. My dad reached his arms down into the pipe, and with a great amount of effort and strength, he yanked me out by my head. Luckily my head stayed attached to my neck. Who knows how long I'd been stuck in that pipe or if I would have ever been discovered if not for Jupiter, "The Wonder Dog," a gift given to us long ago by a fabulous Alpine Cowboy.

When I was about eight years old, my family lived on the Marine Corps base at Quantico, Virginia. My father would often take me and my two brothers, John and Ted (named after baseball great Ted Williams, of course), fishing at a beautiful little spot called Lunga Lake. Sometimes the whole family would go there for picnics or to camp overnight. My dad always made sure that we brought our baseball gloves, and a ball and bat, so that we could play pepper or catch. On one overnight outing, we had just set up our big family tent and my dad began clearing out the grill at our campsite. It was full of charred logs and debris, and when my dad began to pull the logs out he disturbed a big black bumblebee that had been nesting in the fire pit. The bee was mad, and it began aggressively darting around the campground. It swooped down at me and my brothers and it repeatedly dive-bombed my dad. My mother, who was always a little excitable anyway, began screaming in a high-pitch, "Doyle, Doyle, Doyle!" as she herded her young sons out of harm's way and into the tent. We watched the drama unfold through the mosquito netting of the tent as my dad dodged and ducked the angry bumblebee. At one point he reached down and picked a board up off of the ground, and then all of the sudden he just stopped. He slowly lifted the makeshift bat up over his left shoulder and struck a perfect batter's stance. The bumblebee bore down on him like a heat-seeking missile, and it was heading straight for his head. My father remained still and calm. His eye was on the bee. The highly agitated bug became a black blur—a buzzing fastball—and when it came into range, my dad took a furious swing. *Thwack!* The sound of the bee hitting the bat echoed through the campsite as the lifeless lump of insect arced up and out of the park. It was a perfect hit. Not too bad for a pitcher.

My love of journalism and editorial design may have been passed down to me from my father, but I certainly didn't inherit his baseball ability. I played Little League baseball when I was a kid, and I enjoyed

it, but I was never that good at it. When I played Pony League baseball, I was the pitcher once in a tournament, but we didn't go very far up the ladder. In high school I tried out for the baseball team but didn't make the cut. I played basketball instead. My short-lived baseball

career was pretty unremarkable, and I've never really been much of a hard-core baseball fan, but to this day I am still fascinated with the game. When my firstborn son, Patrick (named after my cowboy grandfather and the mule), began playing tee ball, he would squat down in the outfield during a game so that he could watch the ants crawling around under the grass, or he would lie on his back, daydreaming and gazing up at the sky. If a ball happened to be hit out to his field, that was too bad. He couldn't be bothered chasing some silly ball when there were so many other wonderful things to observe in the outfield. My second son, Nick, never caught the baseball fever either. He was always more interested in music. The Most Reverend Harold Stout Sr. would have been pleased.

My two-year-old daughter, Lucy, is athletic and coordinated already, and she may be the one to carry on the baseball tradition in our family—or maybe she'll be a cowboy. One thing I do know for sure, though, is that the Alpine Cowboys will always be a part of her life as they are with my boys.

My children are the descendants of two cowboys, as I am, but in a sense, there has always been a third cowboy in our lives, Herbert Kokernot Jr., the cowboy who loved baseball more than ranching and built a West Texas field of dreams.

Balls and Bees
My brother John (back to viewer) and I, goofing around at Lunga Lake, on the Marine Corps base at Quantico, Virginia, in 1966. The infamous campground barbecue pit, and sometime bumblebee home, can be seen in the background. My dad would often take our family to the lake for picnics and to fish and camp. We always brought a bat, a ball, and our baseball gloves (sometimes worn on our hands). When my brothers and I were growing up, my father couldn't imagine being outdoors with us and not playing catch or a little pepper.

Cowboys and Indians

A ragtag group of baseball players sits for a portrait in 1905. During the early years, the team was known as the Alpine Baseball Team. Alpine has always been ranching country. Located in a desolate region of far West Texas, Alpine became known for its expansive cattle operations and its hardy cowboy culture. But Alpine has also had a real and inexplicably powerful connection to baseball that goes way back. For more than a century the talk of the town has been about baseball. Baseball is a part of Alpine's DNA. The American invention of baseball shares many aspects with the iconic American cowboy. Cas Edwards wrote in the *Alpine Avalanche*: "It is no wonder that ranchmen come from miles around to see the Cats [precursors to the Alpine Cowboys] play ball. There is an air of that old Western hospitality around the park. O. D. Burleson at third base and his brother, Bob, at shortstop, are both actively engaged in ranching, and our crack outfielder and home-run hitter Billie Ward makes his living as active owner and manager of sizeable ranching interests. Outfielders Powers and Thornton can star at ranch life as well as at fielding, throwing and hitting home runs. Pitchers Gaga Llanez, Marselo Alercon and George Zegrafos can twirl a loop as they twirl a baseball. Our big Indian catcher, Chief Riggs, knows his way around a ranch, and when the Chief gets hot behind the bat and lets out a few of his war whoops, fans know that things are going to happen."

Old Rivalry

Horse-drawn wagons and early-model automobiles gather for a baseball game on July 25, 1919, in what is now downtown Alpine. The first Sul Ross Normal College administration building can be seen under construction in the distance. The ball game between Alpine and Marfa was a part of the "Soldiers Welcome Home Day" celebration. Baseball games were organized for every Fourth of July and for just about any other special occasions the locals could come up with. In the early 1900s the population of Alpine was only around 1,200, and there just wasn't much else to do for entertainment. Alpine played baseball games with the neighboring towns, including Fort Stockton, Pecos, Fort Davis, Marathon, Sanderson, and Marfa. Over the years, the Alpine-Marfa games became a hotly contested rivalry. The *Alpine Avalanche* described a game in Marfa between the two teams on July 4, 1903: "The crowd went wild. Men threw their hats in the air and yelled. Women mounted chairs and waved scarves and handkerchiefs." Around 1910 to 1912, with the coming of the Orient Railroad to the area, a baseball team was organized in Alpine called the Orient Team, which was later called the Alpine Blues. In the late 1920s there was a team in Alpine called the Vaqueros. Then in the 1930s the Mexican-American boys in Alpine organized a team that eventually became known as the Alpine Internationals. Interest in baseball in the area dropped off during the Depression and World War II, but when the servicemen began returning home from the war, it was time to play ball again in Alpine. Above: a baseball team from Alpine in 1923.

Nine Lives

The Alpine Cats baseball club strikes a pose for posterity. The owner and manager of the team, C. West, who was the proprietor of the Texas Café, had revived baseball in Alpine in the summer of 1945. His Cats had done fairly well in their first season, losing only one regularly scheduled game out of 12. In January 1946, a meeting was held at West's café to discuss the future of the team. The meeting was presided over by Lloyd Bloodworth, who pointed out the advantage of having a good baseball team in Alpine. "The town must have more recreation and amusements if it is to grow and progress," he said. "People coming here for the scenic and climatic attractions want something to do and places to go. A good baseball team can be made a great attraction to them." At the meeting West announced that plans were under way for a

new baseball park to be located on pastureland given to the town by Herbert Kokernot Jr., owner of the O6 Ranch. Work began in February on the new ballpark, and in March, Cas Edwards wrote about it in his Range Pow-Wow column in the *Alpine Avalanche*: "For 40 years Alpine fans have had hard luck with their baseball parks. In the early days, the ones we put up in the summer were torn down in the winter by folks who found it cheaper to get lumber that way than by going to the yards and buying it. Today things are looking up. The new park now going up just outside the city limits is the best one we ever had. It will be known as Kokernot Field and we are durned sure it won't be stolen or traded out from under us as the other places were."

Cat at Bat

An Alpine Cats player at the plate. In April 1946 the Cats played their first regularly scheduled game of their second season against the Palace Club of El Paso. The Cats played well all season, but in May the owner and manager, C. West, sold the team to Herbert Kokernot Jr., and Ray McNeill was made team captain. Cas Edwards wrote about the new Cats in the *Alpine Avalanche* that month: "Few people realize that the Alpine Cats baseball club is essentially a ranch outfit, but if you check up on its personnel, its ballpark and its general ranch atmosphere, you will find that such is the case. Herbert Kokernot, backer of the Cats, is partner with his father, H. L. Kokernot Sr., in the O6 Ranch which is the best big ranch in Texas." Around that time, this article also appeared in the *Alpine Avalanche*: "Many baseball fans will regret to hear that Mrs. Frankie Eidelberg, sports reporter for the Alpine Cats, has moved from the city. Besides being a very colorful sportswriter, Frankie has won many bathing beauty prizes over the South and West during the past few years."

Giant Two

Cowboys working cattle on Mr. Herbert's 06 Ranch. His huge ranch, which stretched 600 square miles, from Alpine through the Davis Mountains, was, and still is today, a true working cattle operation. The mythic 06 Ranch was rivaled only by the King Ranch in Texas for its size and grandeur. David L. Kokernot, a scout for Sam Houston during the battle of San Jacinto, founded the 06 cattle brand in 1837, when he established a mercantile business and ranch in Gonzales County. His sons, Lee and John, bought land in the Davis Mountains in 1883 to pursue ranching on their own but soon after moved their cattle to Lubbock, Texas. In 1912, after selling his holdings in Lubbock, Lee's son, Herbert Lee Kokernot Sr., returned to the Davis Mountains, bought land, and established the Kokernot 06 Ranch. The ranch was officially owned by Kokernot & Son. Herbert L. Kokernot Sr. eventually turned over all ranching activities to his son, Herbert L. Kokernot Jr., and relocated to San Antonio, where he was prominent in banking and charitable enterprises. He was also president of the First National Bank of Alpine, of which Herbert Jr. was a director.

The Cowboys of Summer

BY NICHOLAS DAWIDOFF

First published as "The Best Little Ballpark in Texas (or Anywhere Else)," Sports Illustrated, July 31, 1989. Reprinted in its original form.

Catching the Fever

In 1946 Herbert Kokernot Jr. (opposite page) took over the Alpine Cats baseball team, which had folded after playing just two games. So it was only natural that a bigger-than-life Texas cattle rancher like Mr. Herbert would name his new baseball club the Cowboys. "There was a fellow running a baseball team in Alpine, and it was about to break up," he said. "I had let him build a park on my land. He was going to quit, so I bought him out, built a nice little ballpark. Our folks out there in Alpine are pretty baseball-minded. I wanted to do something for them. I guess you'd call it civic pride, love of baseball and the kick I get from doing things for those young men." That "nice little ballpark" he spoke of turned out to be a $1.25 million landmark, recognized as the best semipro ballpark in the United States.

One hundred and forty-three miles into the range country southwest of Odessa, Texas, lies the hamlet of Alpine, a cow and college town that 6,800 residents call home. "We're so far out here that nobody thinks anything of driving 100 miles to get some dinner," says cattle rancher Chris Lacy. Alpine is the seat of Brewster County, the largest county in Texas in size (6,169 square miles) and one of the smallest in population (8,000). It is also the heart of the Big Bend region of Texas, so-called for the hard left turn the Rio Grande makes around the Chisos Mountains. The Big Bend is mostly open range, full of javelinas, cactus roses, mule deer, desert willows, and legends, lots of legends.

There is the legend of the Twin Sisters, the pair of notched peaks three miles west of Alpine, named for the two Indian women who loved the same man and quarreled over him so bitterly that the Great Spirit turned them into a two-topped mountain to teach them better manners. And there is the legend of Bobcat Carter, a trapper who put pepper in his shoes to keep his feet warm, subsisted on a diet of prairie dog stew, and lived to be 97 years old.

And there is the legend of the wealthy Alpine cattle rancher who loved both the game of baseball and his hometown with such consuming passion that in 1947 he built what is quite possibly the world's most beautiful ballpark. It was an idea dusted with magic, a summertime daydream of a ball field, surrounded by a 10-foot-high fence of native red stone, with a lush

Bermuda grass outfield, rows of rosebushes, a luxurious manager's bungalow behind third base, and a spectacular vista of the Davis Mountains rising beyond the fences. Like William Randolph Hearst's mansion, San Simeon, the Alpine ballpark was furnished with the choicest materials. Some 1,200 wooden chairs, complete with armrests and the ticket holders' names embossed on the backs, filled the bright green grandstand. The concession stands had roofs made of Spanish tile, and everywhere there were wrought-iron lanterns inlaid with baseball designs. Some of America's famed ballplayers—among them Satchel Paige, Norm Cash, and Gaylord Perry—played there from time to time. But what made all this unusual in terms of West Texas legends is that Kokernot Field is real—as real as its builder, Herbert Kokernot Jr.—and every bit of the story you are about to read is true.

In the 1940s and '50s, most any small town you visited in this part of the country was sure to have certain things: a wide thoroughfare called Main Street, a diner, a honky-tonk bar with Hank Williams songs on the jukebox, and a baseball team. The mid-20th century was the heyday of American baseball; never were there more teams or more ballplayers. Where now the lowest minor league classification, excluding Rookie League, is Class A, in the late 1940s the professional talent reached all the way down to Class D teams. And baseball's popularity was by no means limited to the professional ranks. Towns that weren't big enough to support, say, the Brooklyn Dodgers' third-best Class D

H3046

THE AMAZING TALE OF MR. HERBERT AND HIS

A Rare Breed

Herbert Kokernot's giant 320,000-acre 06 Ranch consisted of 500 sections of outstanding cattle range, with many thousands of head of highly bred white-faced Herefords (left) and a remuda with more than 100 horses. He employed an army of cowboys and support staff for his massive cattle operation. Kokernot was an official of the American Livestock Association and a director of the Texas and Southwestern Cattle Raisers Association. But ranching just supported his baseball habit. Mr. Herbert would routinely release any player who happened to get signed by a big league team, and he would let them keep every cent of any bonus paid. "I sell my cattle, but not my ballplayers," Kokernot often said.

team still had baseball of their own in the form of semipro town teams.

Today, semipro baseball has almost vanished from the land, but 40 years ago it was the best game in many a town. In the West, it meant something truly special. To this day there is an isolation about living in some parts west of the Mississippi. Wide-open spaces can breed an urgency in people to be a part of something—almost anything—social. Attorney Ken Sparks, who grew up in Oklahoma and spent weekends watching games between Alva and Woodward, Oklahoma, recalls, "There was a craving for live entertainment. All week you were out there alone with the land and animals. Come the weekend you were ready to head into town for Saturday night dancing or Sunday afternoon baseball. I still remember the names of all the best ballplayers in Alva."

Some of the players on semipro teams were kids from the local college who hung around for the summer, playing ball and taking dates to the diner. The rest of the team was made up of men who had spent their lives in the town. Having a good town team was a major source of local pride. Baseball as the national pastime was taken with the utmost seriousness, so that having a team that was best in the region or the state was an exciting proposition—like having an extra portion of the American Dream dished out to your hometown.

For some, a winning town team became an obsession. If a man happened to be both extremely wealthy and fervently concerned with the fortunes of the local nine, he might be inclined to help it out a little, perhaps by paying a star pitcher from two counties away to suit up for crucial games. This was perfectly legal in semipro baseball, so if this rich man took it one logical step further and began hiring the best players from the state's colleges to spend their summer vacations playing ball for him, come August he might find he had bought his town a juggernaut. Right there on the local diamond would be a semipro team capable of beating everyone in sight, even capable, perhaps, of holding its own at the annual National Baseball Congress tournament in Wichita. If he kept this up—maybe even went outside the state to lure big-time semipro players to his little town, maybe even plunked down a few hundred per game for a faded major leaguer or two—well, that's how legends were made.

And, the truth was, legends were pretty much the coin of the realm in semipro baseball. The game certainly didn't generate any profit. In fact, there wasn't much to be gained from it unless you liked giving people the pleasure of watching a good game on Sundays and enjoyed the idea that your town might come to be known all across America for its marvelous baseball team.

Of course, if your name was Herbert Kokernot Jr., that was reward enough. Especially if one day 42 years later an old Texan like Flop Parsons would put his feet on the desk in his dusty Alpine real estate office and declare with authority, "Back in the early '50s, semipro baseball in Alpine, Texas, was raised as high as you can get."

It began one summer day in 1946. Kokernot, owner of the O6 (pronounced oh six), one of the largest cattle ranches in Brewster County, had recently agreed to take over the management of the Cats, Alpine's semipro baseball team, and on this day, as he drove the 15 miles from his ranch to Alpine, he was feeling pretty good. He felt good as he passed the white-faced Herefords that grazed on some of the O6's 320,000 acres. He felt good as he surveyed the odd, beautiful shapes of the mountains, greenish-brown in the summer heat. He always felt good about his visits to Alpine. On the hill above town was Sul Ross University, to which Kokernot annually donated bushels of scholarships—one year he handed out 52—so that young Texans might have the opportunity to make something of themselves. In the center of town was the post office, where Kokernot, or Mr. Herbert, as everyone called him, caught up on local news and gossip and received mail related to his substantial holdings in the Pearl and Lone Star breweries and the Fidelity Union Life Insurance Corp. On the edge of town—which in Alpine was very close to the post office—was the ball field he had just taken over.

It hadn't been difficult for Mr. Herbert to convince himself that he should take charge of the team. Since his days with the Alpine Independents, when he had been a smooth-throwing infielder and a .300 hitter, the game had always meant a great deal to him. "He wasn't one of those big, cigar-smoking Texas millionaires," says Byron Brooks, 37, psychology professor and baseball coach at Sul Ross. "Just a little, quiet, unassuming man who didn't feel comfortable in public if he didn't have a necktie on and who loved watching baseball." Mr. Herbert liked it well enough that he bought the Cats to keep baseball in Alpine. The ballpark wasn't much of a structure—crude wooden planks, corrugated tin roof, and chicken wire—but he was so pleased to own it that he painted the red and white O6 brand on the fences.

That day in '46 was special because his father, Herbert Sr., was making his annual summer visit to Alpine. Herbert Sr. had founded the O6 in 1912 and had made it one of the most respected cattle operations in Texas. Herbert Jr. was shy by nature, and he was slightly in awe of his dad. He was a little worried about what Herbert Sr. would think of the ballpark.

Herbert Jr. met Herbert Sr.'s train at the depot, drove the old man through town, past the ballpark, and out to the ranch. If Herbert Sr. had any thoughts regarding his son's purchase, he kept them to himself. Finally, two weeks later, just as Herbert Sr. was about to board a train home, he looked his boy in the eye and said, "Son, if you're going to put the O6 brand on something, do that thing right." Then he climbed on the train and was gone.

It was as though Herbert Jr. had been waiting for those words. He decided Alpine needed a new ballpark, and he chose a tract of O6 land just west of the Sul Ross campus to put it on. He filled his architect's ear with intricate instructions and set him loose. On a visit to Georgia, Mr. Herbert had admired the state's rich, red clay, and so he ordered enough for an infield and had it shipped to Alpine by boxcar. At one point during the four months of construction, a street lamp was in the way of some part of the project. Rather than fuss with the politics of petitioning the town to move the pole, Mr. Herbert bought the whole street and summarily ordered the lamp removed.

Meanwhile, explosives experts blasted red stone out of a makeshift quarry at the O6 ranch, and trucks lugged the stuff to the ballpark. Workmen combed creek beds all over the region, looking for the thickest grass to use as outfield turf. Metalworkers in San Antonio turned out decorative iron baseballs; stitches were painted on them in red. The balls were hung in clusters of three over

Ranch Style

Herbert Kokernot Jr. and John Shell (opposite) at the O6 Ranch. There wasn't a lot of money to be made from semipro baseball, but money was not Mr. Herbert's main motivation for sponsoring the Cowboys. Kokernot was generous with his wealth and good fortune, and he gained a lot of satisfaction from helping his players and the community. Almost every small town in America in the '40s and '50s had a baseball team, but the Cowboys seemed unique and special to the people of Alpine. Cas Edwards, the secretary-treasurer of the team, said it like this: "Some ranchers get their fun out of raising fine horses or cattle. Herbert's hobby is helping to raise fine boys." Below: Mr. Herbert entertains movie actor Monte Hale at the O6 Ranch.

the swinging red entrance gates to the ballpark. Gardeners planted flowers and ivy outside the stadium, and painters covered the outfield wall with a bright blue.

The chief builder was a local man named Junior Gray, who knelt on the Georgia clay and flattened it by hand to make the infield as smooth and seamless as a ballroom floor. One day, a visitor watched Gray laboring on his knees like a scullery maid, and mocked him. Junior looked up calmly and said, "Mr. Herbert told me to do it this way, and if that man told me to make him an infield with an ice cream scoop, I would."

Mr. Herbert stopped by often to see how things were progressing. One day he drove up clutching an envelope. "Twenty thousand dollars from my daddy," he told the workmen. "Guess he thought I was going broke on the ballpark." By the time the last red and white O6 was embedded in the concrete walls of Kokernot Field, the place had cost $1.25 million, a cool million more than had been spent to build Wrigley Field 33 years earlier.

The ballpark was ready in May 1947. Attached to the handsome brick facade at the front entrance to the stadium was a small bronze plaque that read: KOKERNOT FIELD. DEDICATED TO THE PROMOTION OF A CLEAN AND WHOLESOME SPORT, OUR NATIONAL GAME, BASEBALL. On Opening Day, most of Alpine lined up in front of the pretty little ticket booths that stood beside the first and third base stands. The town's wealthier citizens drove their Cadillacs and

Deer Ted

Ted Gray (left) was a legendary cowboy who worked all over the Big Bend country for more than 50 years. His brother, Junior Gray, was the main contractor for Kokernot Field. Ted was also the manager of the O6 Ranch for many years. Ted was a hardworking experienced cowhand, and Kokernot relied on him to run his cattle operation. But Ted was not a baseball fan, and he just didn't understand his boss's obsession with his baseball team. According to Ted Gray's memoir, *Shades of Gray*, Ted was a sportsman in his own way. He was an expert roper, and sometimes he would rope a deer just for the fun of it. Abundant herds of deer and antelope ran on the O6 Ranch, and one time Ted decided to rope a large elk he spotted on the ranch. The experience nearly killed him, and he never attempted it again. Opposite: The living mascot of the Alpine High School Fighting Bucks.

Lincolns through the automobile entrance in right field and parked in a special area along the foul line. There they could watch the game through the windshields and feel secure in the knowledge that if they opened their flasks for a gargle of whiskey, they wouldn't offend any neighbors.

Meanwhile, in the spacious home clubhouse, a group of strapping Texans slipped into crisp red and white uniforms with the team's new name, COWBOYS, sewn across the chest. In previous seasons Alpine players wore the gray and blue uniforms of the Cats, and the team consisted mostly of local ranch hands. But Mr. Herbert, determined to supply Alpine with ballplayers who measured up to his new stadium, had regularly left town in '47 to go talent hunting. He did well, turning up a galaxy of semipro stars such as flashy shortstop Matt Lamarque from Mexia in East Texas and fleet-footed right fielder Billy Ward, who was discovered playing softball up in Corsicana. On Opening Day, the Cowboys defeated the Carlsbad (N. Mex.) Miners. The handwriting was on the wall. Soon the Fabulous Alpine Cowboys, as they came to be known, stood among semipro baseball's elite.

In its very first year the team became the dominant semipro club in the Southwest, winning the two-state regional championship in El Paso and earning a trip to the national tournament. The Cowboys won two and lost two that first time at the nationals, but the fact that such a successful team had emerged from such a small town earned Mr. Herbert the trophy as America's No. 1 sponsor of semipro baseball.

Alpine became so good a baseball town that in 1949 the Cowboys and the Junior Cowboy team, which Mr. Herbert had created so that less talented players from the former Cats wouldn't feel left out, became the two top teams in the Southwest. Over the next decade Alpine was the perennial Southwest champion. The Cowboys never finished higher than third at Wichita, but they were usually in contention.

Meanwhile, Kokernot Field's spring tenant, the Sul Ross Lobos, developed a formidable collegiate program, winning the first NAIA World Series, in 1957. A synergy developed between the Lobos and the Cowboys. The best Sul Ross players, including Cash, a future Detroit Tiger first baseman, played college ball in the spring and then suited up for the Cowboys in the summer, joining other college stars Kokernot had recruited—Baylor's Adrian Burk and Larry Isbell, and Texas A&M's Yale Lary, later a Hall of Fame punter with the Detroit Lions. Mr. Herbert also gave his college players well-

Fly Boys

Mr. Herbert would often commission pilots to fly him and his players to games and tournaments from the remote Big Bend area. In *Shades of Gray*, Ted Gray tells a story about J. O. Casparis, who was a colorful local character and a daredevil pilot. He was frequently hired by the ranchers in the area to shoot eagles from his airplane. Eagles were generally perceived to be a threat to sheep and goats on the ranches. Casparis painted his plane black so that he could sneak up on the big birds without scaring them off, and he rigged his windows to open fully in flight so that he could shoot the eagles from his cockpit. Casparis ended up crashing two of his airplanes, and he was burned badly in one of the accidents. But he continued to fly up into his eighties and eventually died of natural causes. Left to right: Texas governor Allan Shivers, Herbert Kokernot, Marvin O. Kay (local insurance man and away game announcer), J. O. Casparis, and Ray McNeill (Alpine Cowboys manager).

paying jobs on the O6 ranch so they could earn tuition money. Word of this arrangement spread far beyond Sul Ross, and soon Alpine was attracting collegians from all over the country.

Many semipro owners hired good players in the hope of eventually selling them to major league teams at tidy profits. This practice didn't sit well with Mr. Herbert, whose motto was always. "I sell my cattle, but not my ballplayers." He lost thousands of dollars annually, but the professional teams that came knocking always received the same answer from the little man in the cowboy hat: "You pay my players what they deserve or they stay here." Scouts came to respect this attitude. They also respected the fact that Mr. Herbert hired excellent instructors and that he fed and housed his players well.

Eventually, Mr. Herbert developed a nationwide network of contacts who tipped him off about talent. In 1955, for example, Milwaukee Braves scout Gil English telephoned Cowboy manager Tom Chandler and told him about a North Carolina farm boy who could throw hard but needed some seasoning. "Gil," said Chandler, "we have the finest college players in the country playing for us here, and you're asking us to pitch a high school boy?"

"I know," said English. "The Braves will pay his way down, and you just have a look." Soon the Cowboys witnessed the arrival of the greenest, gangliest rookie right-hander Chandler had ever seen. However, the moment the rube got up on the mound everyone forgot about his awkwardness, for Gaylord Perry was a true diamond in the rough. After his season in West Texas, Perry moved up through the minors and eventually racked up 314 major league victories before he retired in 1983. He remembered his summer with Mr. Herbert's Cowboys with gratitude: "I was only a high school kid, playing on a very good team. Some of those guys were former major leaguers. Playing out there in Alpine and staying in the Sul Ross dormitories, that was a special summer."

Mr. Herbert made it worth a ballplayer's while to make his summer home on the range. Besides giving him a job, he set up a standing reward of $100 for a home run, $75 for a triple, and so on. "When he shook hands with you after a game, he usually left something in the handshake," says Parsons, who played shortstop for the Cowboys in 1953 and '54. Following home games Mr. Herbert almost always threw a barbecue and dance for the players and their families at his ranch house. "Of course," says 75-year-old Wally Davis, who managed the Cats from 1942 to '45, "if you made an error, you didn't dare go to that barbecue."

Extreme Makeover

Herbert Kokernot Jr. built his spectacular Kokernot Field in 1947. He had decided to build the new ballpark after his father, on a visit to Alpine, got a glimpse of the shabby ballpark that his son had inherited for his newly purchased team and commented, "Son, if you're going to put the O6 brand on something, do that thing right." From that point on, Mr. Herbert never looked back. He trucked in red granite from a makeshift quarry on the O6 Ranch to construct the walls around the new park, and for the infield, he imported a distinctive red clay he had admired on one of his trips to Georgia. The outfield was groomed with the lushest grass he could find. Kokernot outfitted the new grandstand with 1,200 individual wooden seats—complete with arm rests and the season ticket holders' names printed on the backs—and spacious modern locker rooms underneath. The new ballpark took four months to complete, and when the dust cleared Kokernot had spent a cool $1.25 million on his West Texas field of dreams.

House of Herbert

Mr. Herbert and Gene Russell pose in front of an elaborate ticket window at Kokernot Field. Gene, handsome and always the snappy dresser, became the new General Manager when the Cowboys turned pro and entered the Sophomore League, in 1959. When Kokernot built his new stadium, in 1947, he hired expert ironwork craftsmen in San Antonio to create custom decorative gates and lamp fixtures featuring actual-sized wrought-iron baseballs painstakingly hand-painted white with red stitching and, of course, the ubiquitous 06 brand, which appears in many forms throughout the ballpark. Russell, born and raised in Houston, came from a prominent Texas baseball family. After viewing Kokernot Field for the first time, Gene remarked, "This is one of the finest baseball parks in the nation."

Chandler, a former Texas A&M coach, managed the Cowboys from 1952 to '58 and quickly became almost family to Mr. Herbert. Shortly after Chandler took over the team, Mr. Herbert built his new manager a comfortable cottage beyond third base at Kokernot Field. Says Chandler, 64, who is now a scout for the Cleveland Indians, "One day Mr. Herbert came out to the stadium and saw my car parked outside the house in the rain. He said, 'Tom, you need a garage,' and he built me one of those, too." His generosity extended well beyond baseball. "If I had to guess, I'd say he put more than 700 kids through college, and he never counted the ones who didn't finish four years," says former Cowboy general manager Bud Richards. "There probably wasn't a school in the state that didn't receive money from Mr. Herbert. Of course, he helped anybody who needed it. Once at the El Paso livestock show, he heard about a boy who'd spent a year raising a prize pig only to have it die when the boy got it to the show. Mr. Herbert said, 'We can't have this,' so he bought it for $200. Paying $200 for a dead pig! I guess helping young people kept him young."

On game days the lonely roads from Marfa to the west and Marathon to the east were filled with baseball fans flocking to Kokernot Field to see the Fabulous Alpine Cowboys, and Mr. Herbert did all he could to make it worth the trip. In 1953, when Dodger pitching star Don Newcombe and St. Louis Browns right-hander Bob Turley were stationed at the Brooke Army Medical Center in San Antonio, Mr. Herbert flew the entire Brooke team to Alpine to play the Cowboys. Recalls Newcombe, "Mr. Herbert would give me $100 an inning. Sometimes my arm was very sore, but I made sure I always pitched at least five innings. Later, when I got out of the Army, I used to leave him World Series tickets."

Mr. Herbert sometimes hired major league teams to play one another in exhibitions in Alpine. In 1951, Paige and the Browns took on the Chicago White Sox. Some 6,000 people jammed the place to see Paige. "He only pitched an inning," says Brooks, "but even now I can find you 20 old-timers around Alpine who will swear Satchel Paige struck them out that day." Before the game Paige told Mr. Herbert that he very much liked his cowboy hat. Shortly thereafter all the Browns players were quietly asked their hat sizes. A phone call was placed to Fort Worth, and a load of quality headgear was flown to the 06 in time to be passed out at the postgame cookout. "It wasn't a show of wealth," says Chandler. "Mr. Herbert was actually very timid. He just loved to make people happy."

When slick-fielding White Sox shortstop Chico Carrasquel heard Mr. Herbert announce his customary monetary prizes for hits, he asked, "How much for an assist?"

"Twenty-five dollars," Mr. Herbert replied immediately. He then turned to a friend and asked, "What's an assist?"

Chris Lacy, Mr. Herbert's grandson, says, "I think he liked baseball people even more than he liked the game."

That may have been true, but there was no question about Mr. Herbert's competitive nature when it came to the game. After Alpine qualified for the 1956 tournament at Wichita, Mr. Herbert heard that several other teams were padding their rosters with major leaguers picked up from military bases around the country. So Chandler was given permission to sign right-hander Jack Sanford of the Philadelphia Phillies, future White Sox pitcher Joel Horlen, and future Dodgers slugger Carl Warwick.

At the same time Mr. Herbert also delivered on a promise he had made in the Brooklyn clubhouse after the Dodgers' 1955 World Series victory. He had pushed his way up to the Series hero, pitcher Johnny Podres, congratulated him, and said, "I want you to come down to Texas sometime and pitch for us."

"I can't just pitch for every hick town in America that wants me to," Podres responded. Whereupon Mr. Herbert informed him, "I'll make it worth your while," and whispered some figures in his ear.

"When do you want me?" asked Podres.

The answer turned out to be the summer of '56, when Podres was due to go into the Navy. "He flew me out to Wichita and gave me a thousand bucks, plus 100 dollars a strikeout, to pitch for him," says Podres. "That was more money than I made with the Dodgers. I struck out seven guys in four innings, and they wanted me to pitch again, but the Navy wouldn't let me."

In general, though, Mr. Herbert disliked the idea of putting major leaguers in Cowboy pinstripes. "I was mostly restricted to using college kids," says Chandler. "He told me, 'If I wanted to run a pro team, I'd buy the Yankees.'"

In 1958 Mr. Herbert decided to put lights in Kokernot Field. Before installing them, he toured lighted ballparks all over Texas to be sure that his field would have more bulbs than any other in the state. "He told the contractor, 'I want lights better than Yankee Stadium's,'" says Cats second baseman Ray McNeil. "It didn't matter to him what they cost."

Best Ticket in Town

The day of a big game in Alpine was like a national holiday. There was an electricity in the air. People would gather in the cafés to talk about batting averages and to debate the outcome of the upcoming contest. Businesses would close up early and everyone would head to the ballpark. Sure, it was a ranching community with a rich heritage of cowboy culture, but at the end of the day Alpine was a baseball town, through and through. The townsfolk were knowledgeable about the local baseball scene, and they kept up with baseball on a national level as well. The town supported the team because the team gave back to them. The game of baseball shares aspects with cowboy and ranching culture that resonated with West Texans in the '40s and '50s. They each have a strong work ethic and an innate quality of all-American wholesomeness. A bronze plaque that Mr. Herbert mounted on the wall at the entrance to the ballpark is inscribed with these words: "Kokernot Field. Dedicated to the promotion of a clean and wholesome sport, our national game, baseball."

H101

Hot Game

View of the grandstand from center field during a Cowboys game. In the '50s, the West Texas region was going through a legendary drought. It could get very hot on game days—Alpine is in the desert, after all—but the crowds at Kokernot Field were constantly exceeding the turnouts in some of the larger baseball markets. During that period, before lights were installed in the ballpark, eventually providing cooler night games, men would show up in the midday West Texas heat wearing their finest workday suits and long-sleeved shirts fully buttoned up. Women often wore long dresses and gloves, and everybody wore hats. On special occasions the crowds were so large that extra bleachers were brought in that stretched all the way down the first and third baselines out to, and sometimes past, the outfield walls.

The following year, against his better instincts, Mr. Herbert became the president of a professional minor league baseball team. Southwestern semipro baseball was dying. With the end of the Korean War, the Army had ceased sponsoring the service teams that had long been an important element of semipro competition. Bad times in the oil business eliminated another major group of sponsors. The Cowboys were running out of teams to play. When the Boston Red Sox offered to make Alpine the smallest town to have a pro team by giving it a franchise in the Class D Sophomore League, Mr. Herbert said he would give it some thought. The Red Sox were willing to call the team the Cowboys. They even agreed to keep the outfield fences free of advertising, which would make the field perhaps the only ballpark of its kind in the minors.

So Mr. Herbert gave it a go. With future Angel All-Star shortstop Jim Fregosi and Red Sox third baseman Dalton Jones on the roster, the Cowboys won the first Sophomore League title. There were things, however, about these 'fessionals, as he called them, that Mr. Herbert couldn't abide. In the old days when a slight rainfall softened his infield, Mr. Herbert had simply called the game off, telling ticket holders to use their stubs the next day. You couldn't do that with pros. McNeil remembers, "He told me, 'I'm fed up with this 'fessional baseball. Why, they trade these boys right and left, selling them off like cattle.'"

Mr. Herbert wasn't entirely displeased when the league folded after three years. Before this happened, however, he and his ballpark spun their usual spell over ballplayers. "It was amazing," says Fregosi, who played 18 years in the majors. "The best ballpark I ever played in."

With the Cowboys defunct, for the next seven years Kokernot Field was the exclusive home of the Sul Ross Lobos. In a sense, Alpine adopted the Lobos as their new town team. Mr. Herbert, of course, became their most enthusiastic supporter. Then in 1968, as the team returned from losing in the first round of the NAIA World Series, word was passed down the bus aisle that Sul Ross president Norman McNeil was discontinuing the baseball program. McNeil had never had much use for athletics, or for Mr. Herbert. "Apparently he thought a college ought to concentrate everything on academics," says Brooks. "He also might have been a little jealous of Mr. Herbert and the attention he got."

In Alpine there was outrage. "Mr. Herbert never interfered, never made his donations with strings attached," says Chandler. "He gave tuition money to people who needed it whether they could play baseball or not. He gave that school so much, and all he ever cared about was a boy's education, seeing a good game, and being sure that his cows were eating." Despite howls of protest, the school held firm. So Mr. Herbert gave the field to Alpine High School, making it the nation's most lavish high school diamond. After that he wasn't seen around town as much.

Fifteen years went by. Without Mr. Herbert, the ballpark fell into disrepair. "He was just sick about it," says Chandler. "The lamps were falling down, everything needed paint, seats were in disarray. He was hurt and offended that nobody kept it up. He was really down."

Then in the fall of 1983, wonderful news arrived with the cactus roses. President McNeil was gone, and the weekly *Alpine Avalanche* reported that college base-ball was returning to the Big Bend. Sul Ross leased the ballpark again and spent $150,000 planting, painting, polishing, and generally restoring things to their former splendor. The school also hired Brooks, a coach who appreciated Alpine baseball wisdom and the adage that went, "Visiting teams never do very well the first time they come to Kokernot Field. Their mouths are hanging open at the sight of our ballpark."

Mr. Herbert consented to throw out the first ball at the Lobos' home opener in 1983, but he was reluc-tant to get his hopes up, and he stayed away after that. In 1987, at age 87, he died and was buried on a knoll on the O6 range in view of the ranch house, the fences, and the cottonwoods that chase along toward the mountains and beyond to the ballpark he had built 40 years before.

These days, after the college season is over, the loveliest ballpark in America becomes home to the Alpine Pony League team, coached by Scotty Lewis, who, like his father before him, went to college on a baseball scholarship paid for by Herbert Kokernot Jr. On Lewis's squad is a hard-hitting, smooth-fielding first baseman named Lance Lacy. He is the great grandson of Mr. Herbert and the first Kokernot to play for a team on the family field. Lance, 14, is a freckled little fellow with a bright grin. Watching him smack a line drive or deftly field a twisting grounder would have brought joy to his great-grandfather's heart. As former Cowboy shortstop Pete Swain says, "Mr. Herbert would have been so elated to actually have somebody in the family playing there, where Gaylord Perry and Norm Cash played. That would have made all the time and money and hurt worthwhile. People in Alpine still talk as though he's looking down on Kokernot Field, protecting it, and if he is, I think he's smiling again."

Going Pro

Herbert Kokernot at home plate catches the first pitch, tossed by Grady Terry, a Midland oilman and president of the Sophomore League, to open the league's 1959 season. It was a gala day at Kokernot Field, as practi-cally half the town of Alpine, 2,500 fans, turned out for the Cowboys' inaugural game as a farm team for the Red Sox. It was an impressive day for the Cowboys debut: They were the smallest town in professional ball, and they plastered the San Angelo Pirates, 18–1. Standing on the mound is Don Schwall, who was the starting and win-ning pitcher for Alpine. "The Pirates looked lousy but this isn't taking anything away from the Cowboys," wrote Jim O'Brien in the *Big Bend Sentinel*. "They would have looked good against the New York Yankees." Within three years, Kokernot and the Red Sox called it quits and the league folded.

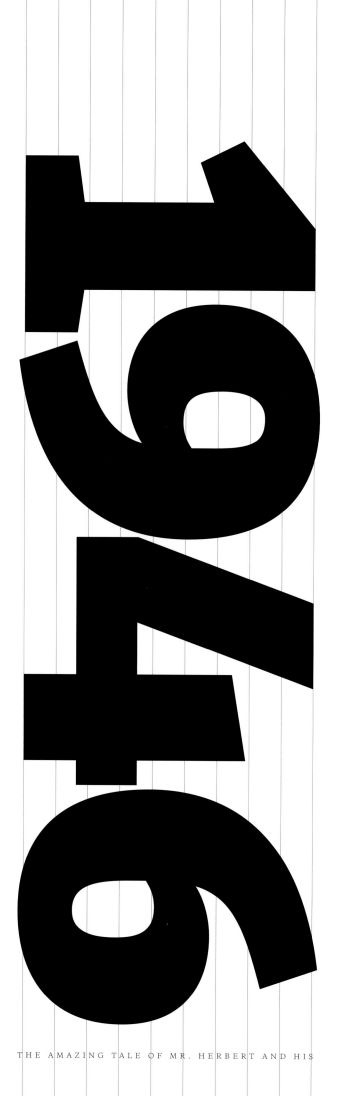

1946

First Up

The inaugural game of the brand-new Alpine Cowboys baseball club was in June 1946 against the Salty Dogs, an all-black team from Fort Stockton. The Cowboys beat the Salty Dogs 12–2. Ray McNeill, the Cowboys' first baseman and team captain, had a field day at bat, with three hits and a walk out of five times up, scoring three of the Cowboys' 12 runs. Second baseman Bob Burleson hit a home run in the fourth inning, scoring two of his teammates. Every member of the Cowboy club saw action in the game except Manager O. D. Burleson. The *Alpine Avalanche* reported, "Zagrafos, Cowboy southpaw, was in fine fettle, whiffing nine of the Dogs in five innings when he was called away from the game by pressing business." Below: The first Alpine Cowboys baseball club photographed with umpires and other officials at the original Kokernot Field. Herbert Kokernot Jr. is standing in the back row, third from left. This is one of the rare photos of Mr. Herbert wearing a baseball cap instead of his signature Open Road Stetson cowboy hat. Standing, left to right: Cas Edwards, Nig Bennett, Herbert Kokernot Jr., Truman Hatch, Frank Young, Bill Dorris, W. E. Vannoy, and Jug Harris Sr. Kneeling, left to right: D. C. Moore, Billy Weston, Burr Thornton, Lloyd Henderson, Freddy Davis (batboy), Bud Powers, Charlie Davis, John D. Harris, Lefty Miller, and Ross Moore. Sitting, left to right: Bobby Wuest, Billy Ward, Wally Davis, O. D. Burleson, Bob Burleson, Travis Cook, Lefty Smith, and Ray McNeill. Front, left to right: Eddie Burling and Don Burleson (batboys).

Home on the Range

The Alpine Cowboys warm up before a game in front of a capacity crowd at the original Kokernot Field. The new Cowboys club inherited the ballpark from the Cats, who had built it on Kokernot's land just north of town. C. West, the former owner of the Cats, had planned to build a modern ballpark, enclosed with 1,460 feet of new fence and a grandstand with seating for more than 1,000 people. It was to have bright, clean dressing rooms and showers, and lights were to be installed for night games. Work on the new field was suspended for several weeks, however, because of a tie-up of building materials. The shortage of materials continued to hold up progress on the new park, so when the 1946 season began, the new fence had been completed but only a part of the stands was ready. Even so, Mr. Herbert was so excited about his new baseball team that he could overlook the shabby facility, made of old boards and chicken wire, that was to be the new home of his Alpine Cowboys baseball club. After all, it was nicer than any ballpark that had been built in the Alpine area up to that point. He had the words "Kokernot Field Home of the Cowboys" painted on a rickety wooden sign, which was mounted above the entrance to the makeshift stadium.

¡Aye, Chihuahua!

In August 1946, the Cowboys and more than 70 supporters from Alpine (right) drove south to Chihuahua City for a three-game series. The Northern Mexican metropolis met the Alpine contingency with much fanfare. The series had been heavily promoted in Chihuahua City, and the Cowboys learned that they had been the first all-Anglo team to play a tournament there. On the first morning, the Alpine group was taken on a sightseeing tour, and that night they were treated to a festive dinner and dance. The Cowboys didn't end up winning the tournament, but the whole experience of the trip was unforgettable. In an article that appeared in the *Alpine Avalanche* after the trip, Cas Edwards (top row center, holding hat) reported, "We pasted our Cowboy Club stickers all the way from here to Chihuahua and back and when we arrived in Juárez on our return trip we saw cars driving around with Cowboy stickers on them."

Babe on the Border

The Cowboys won the first game of the Chihuahua series 4–3, and Mr. Herbert threw out the ceremonial first ball in the second game (pictured below). Alpine won that game handily 9–0, which set them up for the championship game. In the *Alpine Avalanche* Cas Edwards described the scene: "Before the largest crowd of the series, the Cowboys faced the Avalos, or Smelter Club, Sunday afternoon, for the third and last game. Dressed in beautiful costumes, the queens of the Chihuahua clubs were there to meet Mrs. Babe Crawford (opposite), who was the queen of the Alpine Cowboys. With camera shutters clicking and the band playing, they marched across the baseball field with numerous attendants in a ceremony of joy and goodwill, in which the queen of the Alpine Cowboys was presented with a beautiful engraved baseball trophy in honor of our visit to their city. After that our queen threw the first ball across home plate and the game was on."

Big Ball in Cowtown

The Cowboys had a remarkable run for a new team, closing out their first season with a record of 19 wins and eight losses. Cas Edwards wrote in the *Alpine Avalanche*, "The Cowboys turned in their uniforms and disbanded. Members of the team, all of whom give their time to the team without recompense, felt that they could not afford to stay away from their businesses or jobs further this season." On a Saturday night following the last home game, Mr. Herbert entertained the team with a lavish steak dinner and dance at the Holland Hotel. Speeches were made, and then Kokernot (front row, center) presented the team with custom-made jackets. The jackets were reversible, with one side in brown gabardine and the other side in red and white flannel. A hand-sewn patch with the insignia of the 1946 Alpine Cowboys was affixed to the front.

COWBOY TALES Charlie Davis, shortstop

The beginning of baseball in Alpine was in 1946, when the Alpine military men were returning home from World War II. Alpine was a small town, with nothing to do. Mr. C. West, owner of the Texas Café, organized a baseball team called the Alpine Cats. The Alpine Cats played teams from many surrounding towns, including teams in New Mexico. Several Alpine boys joined the team, including me.

In June 1946 Herbert Kokernot became interested in baseball and purchased the Alpine Cats from Mr. West. He then changed the name to the Alpine Cowboys. All the Alpine Cats players agreed to play baseball for Mr. Kokernot. Mr. Kokernot gave many scholarships to Sul Ross students who played baseball for him. He had so many good ballplayers, he had to organize two teams, the Alpine Cowboys and the Alpine Junior Cowboys, as he did not want to let any of his players go.

I played baseball for Mr. Kokernot from 1946 to 1953. I had the pleasure of going to Chihuahua, Mexico, to play in a baseball tournament in 1946. Mr. Kokernot also took the Alpine Cowboys to the Wichita, Kansas, National Semipro Baseball tournament in 1947, after winning all the games in the El Paso tournament. On January 4, 1946, Mr. Kokernot gave a dinner and dance at the Holland Hotel for all of his baseball players, where he presented them with Alpine Cowboys jackets and sweaters. I can still remember that wonderful evening, and I still have that sweater.

Dancing with the Stars

Charlie Davis and other Alpine Cowboys players and supporters dance the night away at the Holland Hotel celebration. The next day Mr. Herbert invited the team, officials, and other supporters to the 06 Ranch for a deer hunt. When the hunt was completed Sunday night, the group had killed 14 black-tailed bucks, most of them eight to 10 points and weighing up to 200 pounds. Kokernot announced that he had plans to improve Kokernot Field before the next season. New grass was to be planted, and he was lining up materials to build a spectacular new and improved ballpark.

Batter Up

Prior to the 1947 season, Mr. Herbert rounded up the best architects and craftsmen he could find to build his dream park, the likes of which had never been seen anywhere in the region. O6 Ranch foreman Ted Gray's brother, Junior, was hired as the main contractor for the new stadium. Kokernot spared no expense to build the highest quality ballpark that could be built at the time, spending nearly $75,000 at the outset. This time he wanted to make sure that the Kokernot name could be proudly displayed on the new home of his beloved Alpine Cowboys baseball club. Below: A Cowboys player takes a stand in the recently completed Kokernot Field.

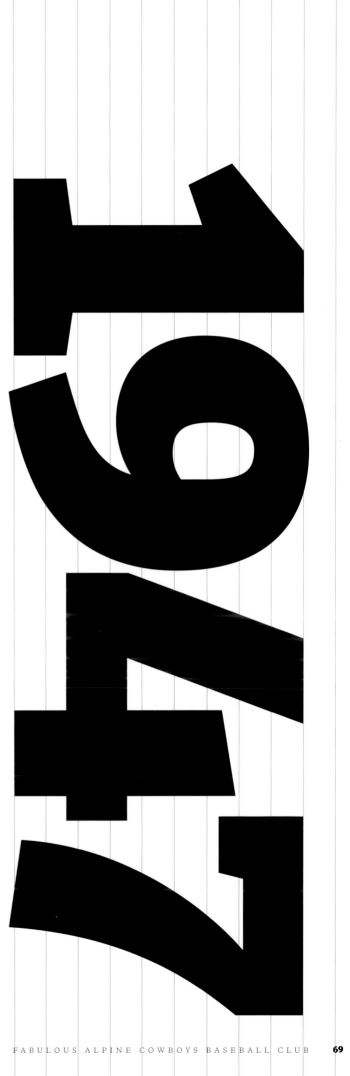

Play Ball!

In May 1947, the spectacular modern version of Kokernot Field was ready for its unveiling. The opening game of the season was a doubleheader against the Carlsbad, New Mexico, Miners. A large enthusiastic crowd showed up to get its first glimpse of the ballpark and the new edition of the Alpine Cowboys. A number of new players had joined the team, including several Sul Ross College boys. The state-of-the-art grandstand, which was mostly completed by game time, and the lush new sod infield were the stars of the show. Featuring the latest in stadium seating (workers installing the seats, above), the new concrete and steel grandstand could now accommodate 1,000 people comfortably. Beneath the stands were modern locker rooms with hot showers, public rest rooms, ticket offices, and two concession stands. The Cowboys won the season opener, defeating the Carlsbad team 2–0. Lefty Ray Miller pitched a steady and impressive first outing for the Cowboys, with ten strikeouts. He got excellent support throughout the game from his new teammates. Meanwhile, the Junior Cowboys lost their opening game of the season against Presidio at the border town's not-so-modern ballpark. In contrast to the proud Kokernot Field debut, at the Presidio game, swirling dust partially obscured the field and caused numerous errors.

Train to Wichita

A beaming Herbert Kokernot and his Alpine Cowboys are met by official greeters in cowboy duds as they arrived by train for the 1947 National Baseball Congress. The annual tournament, at Lawrence Field in Wichita, Kansas, decided the National Champion in the semipro ranks. The Cowboys had played well all season and were the winners of the Southwestern Semipro Tournament in El Paso. Now, in mid-August, they were set to take on the best teams in the nation. Mr. Herbert had arranged for a special Pullman train car to transport the team and a large group of Alpine fans to Wichita. Some additional players had been taken along to strengthen the team, as permitted by the tournament rules. They included second baseman Martin Mehall from Alamogordo, New Mexico, who was voted most valuable player in the El Paso tournament, right-handed pitcher Cowboy Thornton, and Happy Spangler, both from Hurley, New Mexico. The Alpine Cowboys had received a lot of publicity prior to the tournament, and they had become the darlings of sportswriters covering the event, describing them "as one of the most colorful teams in the annual classic." The team received more than a hundred telegrams from well-wishers on the eve of their opening game of the tournament, including one from Texas governor Beauford Jester.

At the Tourney

Mr. Herbert and the team pose for a photograph in Wichita. The Cowboys had gotten off to a flying start in their first game of the National Baseball Congress Tournament, or "Tourney," as Kokernot would say, defeating the powerful Camp Lee, Virginia, Travelers 9–5. But in their second game, the Cowboys were overwhelmed by the Colorado champions, The Golden Coors, by the embarrassing score of 20–0. It was one of the most lopsided games in National Semipro tournament history. The Golden Coors pitcher, Don Swartz, mowed down the Alpine batters with machinelike precision. Mercifully, a tournament ruling halted the contest at the end of several innings. In the third game, behind the strong two-hit pitching of Cowboy Thornton, the Cowboys bounced back, with a 6–0 win over the Kirksville, Missouri, Red Roosters. Completely shaking off the effects of the second-round trouncing at the hands of The Golden Coors, the Cowboys got the jump on the favored Roosters and pounded the ball solidly. In the fourth-round game, the Cowboys faced the Jacksonville, Florida, Terminal Railroaders, one of the strongest teams in the tournament. Loose defensive play led to a 6–0 loss by the Cowboys, and the team was eliminated from the Tourney.

Local Heroes

Back in Alpine, the townsfolk felt that even though the Cowboys had been eliminated from the tournament before getting into the final rounds, they had made an excellent showing. Alpine had gone up against the best semipro baseball players in the nation and had left Wichita with their pride intact. When the Cowboys returned home, they were met by a royal reception. A large delegation of fans had driven to Fort Stockton to meet the team at the train station, and then they were given a Highway Patrol escort back to Alpine. When the Cowboys pulled up to the south entrance of Sul Ross College, they were met by another cheering throng of fans and the high school band. A parade that included city fire trucks, American Legion representatives, and the players in cars and a jeep wound its way from the college through town to the Holland Hotel, where city officials gave the Cowboys an official welcome home. Banners bearing the words "Well Done, Cowboys" were strung across Holland Avenue. Mr. Herbert expressed his appreciation for the fine reception. "It was entirely unexpected, and we were overwhelmed by this demonstration," he said. "We did our best at the National Tournament, and we deeply appreciate the backing and encouragement received from Cowboys fans."

The First Noel

At the end of the 1947 season, the Cowboys' first full schedule, the team had made a name for itself and found a place in the hearts of the Alpine community. That didn't keep some of the press from taking a few shots, however. Pete Lightner wrote in the *Wichita Eagle*: "The wealthy Cowboys' sponsor, Herbert Kokernot Jr., who has more ranches than Notre Dame has halfbacks, has his own baseball park. He had in fact everything but a good team this year." The 50-year-old Kokernot was not discouraged by any of the critics. He had caught the baseball fever. The excitement of going to the national tournament and the accolades the team had received from its first full season energized him. He had a brand new half-million-dollar ballpark that was the envy of the league. This was fun. In December, Mr. Herbert was named Sponsor of the Year by the National Baseball Congress in Wichita, Kansas. That was just icing on the cake.

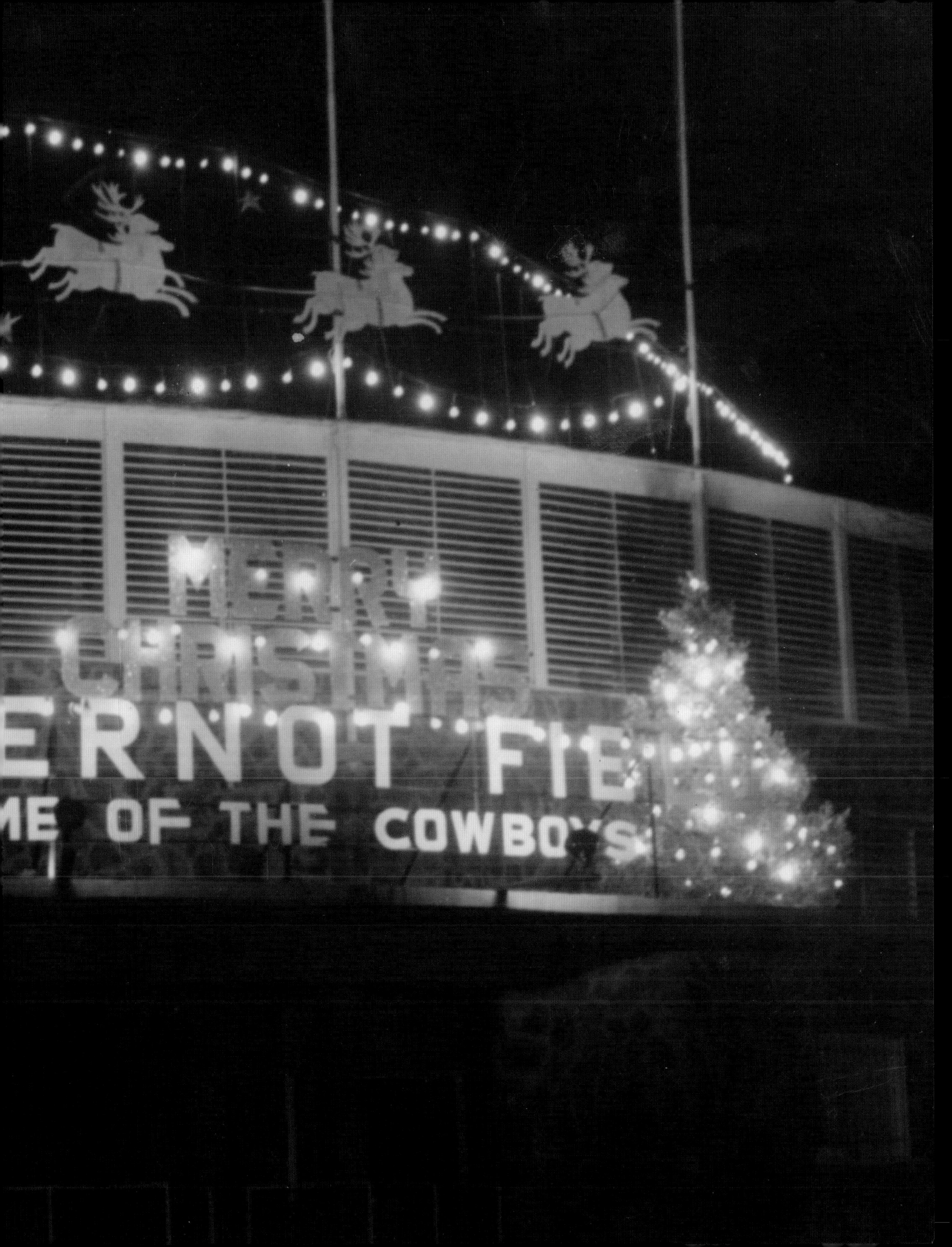
MERRY
ERNOT FIE
ME OF THE COWBOYS

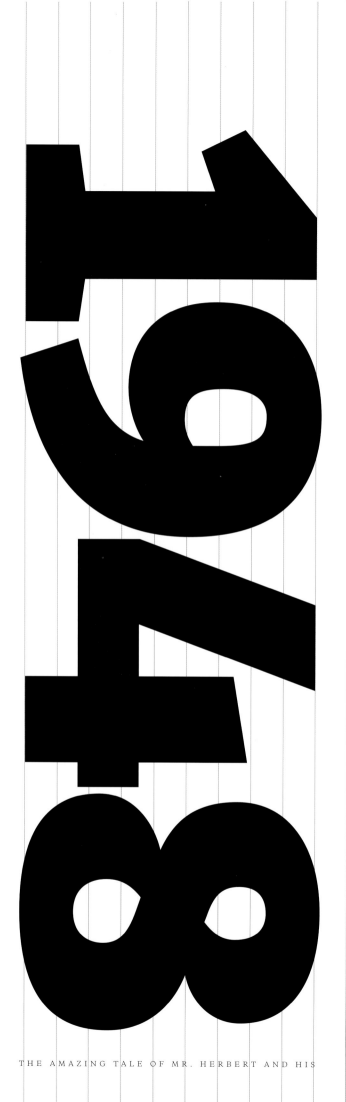

1948

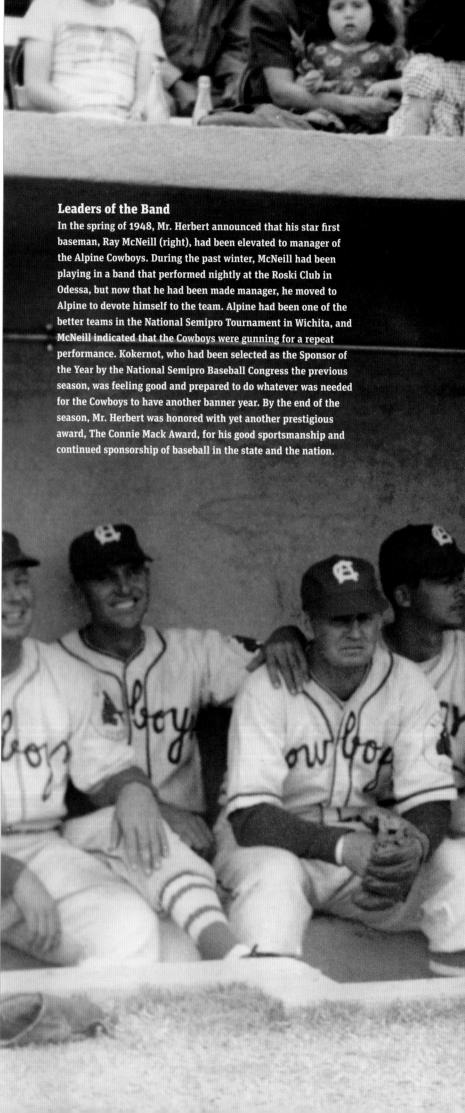

Leaders of the Band

In the spring of 1948, Mr. Herbert announced that his star first baseman, Ray McNeill (right), had been elevated to manager of the Alpine Cowboys. During the past winter, McNeill had been playing in a band that performed nightly at the Roski Club in Odessa, but now that he had been made manager, he moved to Alpine to devote himself to the team. Alpine had been one of the better teams in the National Semipro Tournament in Wichita, and McNeill indicated that the Cowboys were gunning for a repeat performance. Kokernot, who had been selected as the Sponsor of the Year by the National Semipro Baseball Congress the previous season, was feeling good and prepared to do whatever was needed for the Cowboys to have another banner year. By the end of the season, Mr. Herbert was honored with yet another prestigious award, The Connie Mack Award, for his good sportsmanship and continued sponsorship of baseball in the state and the nation.

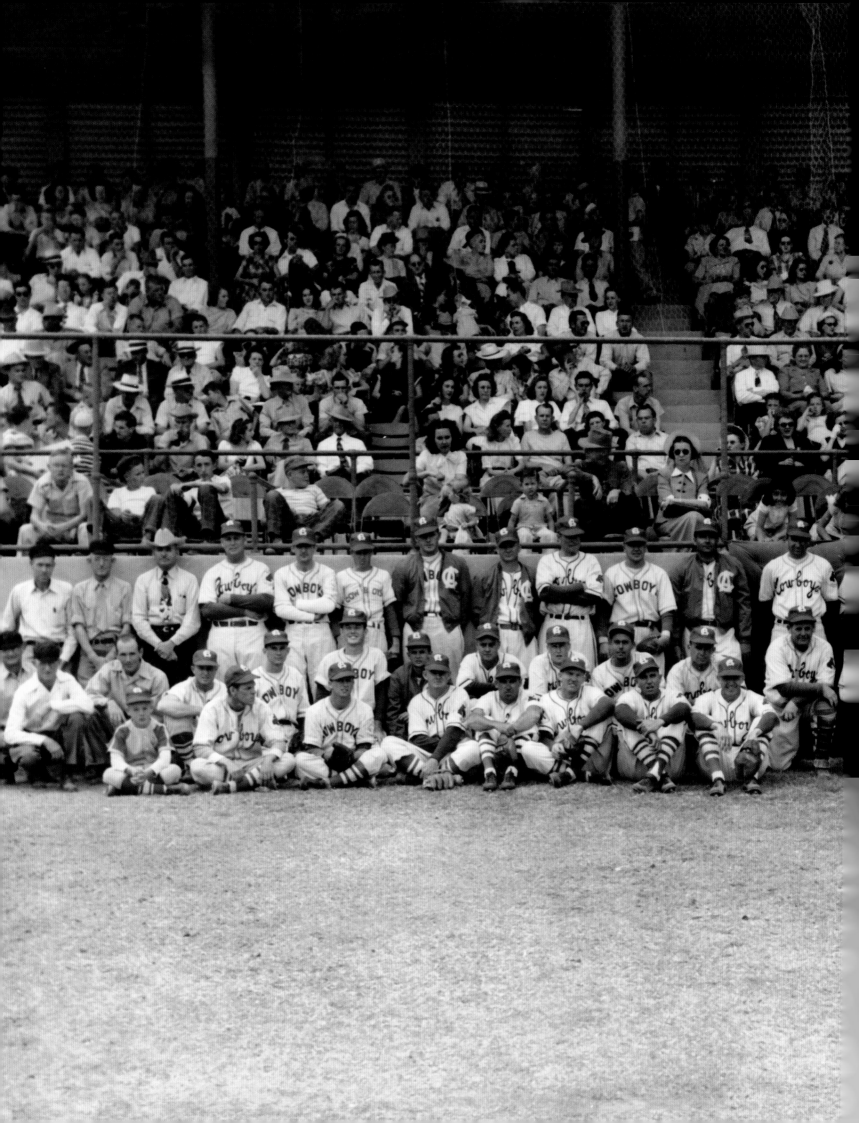

Hairy Opener

The famous House of David baseball club opened the 1948 season, with two games against the Cowboys. The colorful team from Beaton Harbor, Michigan, had been touring all over the U.S. and Canada since 1935. The Davids were known for their distinctive long beards and their entertaining pepper ball performances. Some of the players had never cut their hair or shaved their beards. Their shaggy looks really stood out in the clean-cut conformity of 1948. Despite their outward appearances, the Davids were a clean-living bunch. The team was affiliated with the National Semipro Baseball Congress, and they provided a classy crowd-pleasing game of baseball. Before the first highly anticipated game, the Cowboys and the House of David players were paraded down the streets of Alpine, with a marching band leading the way and business leaders and schoolchildren waving from cars. The biggest baseball crowds ever seen in Alpine turned out for the two games, and the large main grandstand was filled to capacity and running over into the sideline bleachers. The Cowboys won the first game 11–6 and lost the second game 11–1.

COWBOY TALES Glenn Eaves, local fan

I grew up in Alpine and went to most of grade school there. I graduated from Alpine High School in 1954 and graduated from Sul Ross in 1958, 1959.

Every year the Cowboys would play the House of David team. They all wore long beards, which looked a little strange, but, man, they could play baseball. Sometimes Alpine won, and sometimes they didn't.

One time I remember seeing the Cowboys play Holloman AFB, and Mr. Kokernot had a contest to see if anyone could throw a baseball over the center-field fence, about 420 feet—same as today. He offered a prize of $100. Many of the players tried from behind home plate, but none could do it. Just when it looked like the prize money wouldn't be claimed, a tall, lanky black outfielder for Holloman wound up and took a javelin-type run from behind home plate. He threw it right over the center-field fence, clearing it by about ten feet. I don't know how far he threw it. One hundred dollars was a lot of money back in those days. I've never seen a major leaguer throw one that far.

Mr. Kokernot was one of the finest men who ever lived. He quietly did many things for the city—gave the land next door to the stadium and had the stadium for little leaguers built. He used to provide the uniforms and other equipment for the Alpine High School team when I was in school, plus he gave baseball scholarships to Sul Ross. He provided all the beef for the Paisano Baptist encampment every year, and hundreds attended. My friend Jack Richardson and I had a little ole band back in the late 50s, and we used to play at the American Legion quite often. Mr. Kokernot was usually there, and if it looked like we were going to have a small gate, he'd come over and say, "You boys going to make any money tonight?" Sometimes we'd say, "Not much, Mr. Kokernot." He'd put in a 20-dollar bill, which was equivalent to $100 today. What a wonderful guy.

First Shot

During the off-season, Mr. Herbert added a few more top-notch talents to the Cowboys roster and he made some additional improvements to Kokernot Field. In March, Cas Edwards wrote in the *Alpine Avalanche*: "In between sub-zero blizzards from the north and dust storms from the west, workmen are busy preparing Kokernot Field for faster baseball and more comfort for the fans. The field is being leveled and grassed, hot and cold showers are being installed in the dressing rooms, bleachers to seat about 300 are being installed, the grandstand and fences are being touched up with fresh paint and more parking room added down the third base line for visitors who want to see the game from their automobiles." Jedge Winkle of the *San Antonio Express* wrote: "Alpine now boasts the finest baseball plant in Texas for towns under 50,000 population, thanks to Kokernot's determination to build the game up, and the fans of Alpine make no secret of the fact that they think Kokernot is driving for a franchise for Alpine in some pro league." The Cowboys lost their first regularly scheduled game of the 1948 season to the Carlsbad, New Mexico, Miners. In that game, Cowboys manager Ray McNeill used 16 men from his squad, trying to find a combination that clicked.

Back to Wichita

In June, the Cowboys played a highly anticipated game against their longtime rival just down the road, the Marfa Indians. Leading up to the game, this appeared in the *Alpine Avalanche*: "Mr. Kokernot facetiously requests all Marfa and Alpine baseball enthusiasts to be present with their brass knuckles and other weapons of offense or defense to root and 'fight' for their favorites." A crowd of 1,200 wildly cheering fans showed up for the game, which was dedicated to the old-time baseball players of Alpine. The game was a hard-fought contest, but in the end the Marfa team won bragging rights by beating the Cowboys 3–2. The Cowboys steadily improved as the season progressed, though, and when it was time to play in the Southwestern Semipro Tournament in El Paso, the team really had hit their stride. The Cowboys were undefeated throughout the meet, clinching the championship with a 5–3 win over the Fort Bliss Falcons. It was the first time in the tournament's history that a defending champion had repeated the feat. After the Fort Bliss game, Mr. Herbert announced that the Cowboys were heading to the "Little World Series" in Wichita for the second year in a row. As an incentive, he informed his players that on top of their normal $20-a-day salaries, they would receive bonuses of $250 each if they could win the first three games of the National Semipro Tournament, and on top of that, he would divide the $10,000 purse for winning the Championship equally among the 16 players if they could win the whole thing. Kokernot wanted to win badly, and he put his money where his mouth was.

The New Jersey Kokernots

The colorful Alpine Cowboys had been favorites to win the National Semipro Baseball Tournament. Prior to the meet, Mr. Herbert had promised his players everything but the moon to win the championship. A large contingency of Cowboys fans made the trip to Kansas, and the entire town of Alpine eagerly listened to the games on the radio back at home. Regardless of the hype, the Cowboys lost their first game 3–1 to the Fort Benning, Georgia, Doughboys, and were quickly eliminated from the tournament in their second game, losing to the Camden, Arkansas, Krafts-men 4–3. Despite his disappointment, Mr. Herbert gathered up his players, their wives, and supporters and took them all on a vacation to Colorado Springs. When the Cowboys arrived back to town, Mr. Herbert invited the Fort Benning team to Kokernot Field for a rematch. He paid the team's way to Alpine and then capped the whole event off with a big barbecue at the O6 Ranch. Meanwhile, back in Wichita, the Tydols, an underdog team from Glenridge, New Jersey, had unexpectedly won its first game of the National Tournament but then discovered it didn't have enough money to continue tournament play. When Mr. Herbert heard that the team was going to withdraw, he told the Tydols' manager that he would take care of all expenses as long as the team remained in the running for the championship. When Kokernot found the eastern team sleeping on cots in nonair-conditioned rooms, he made arrangements to move them into his team's first-class ac-commodations. The Glenridge ballplayers, who had begun calling themselves The Kokernots, ended up winning fourth place in the tournament. At the award ceremony in Wichita (above), Koker-not accompanied Tydols manager Johnny Dale to home plate to accept the trophy. Asked to say a few words to the 9,000 fans in the stands, the "baseball-minded angel," Mr. Herbert, first complimented the New Jersey team, then added: "Next year, I am planning to bring a club here that will take the title back to Texas, where it belongs."

THE AMAZING TALE OF MR. HERBERT AND HIS

Big Show

In March Mr. Herbert used his newfound influence in the baseball world to bring big league baseball to Alpine. Kokernot had arranged for the Chicago Cubs and the St. Louis Browns to play an exhibition game at Kokernot Field. The little baseball-crazed town eagerly awaited the arrival of the big day. An article in the *San Angelo Standard Times* reported: "Excitement over the prospect of witnessing the first big league game ever played in a 'cow-town' Alpine's size is beyond belief. Mrs. Bonnie Newell, city librarian, provided Alpine youngsters with printed data regarding each of the big league players, then conducted a 'Quiz Kid' session the next day with results that were no less amazing."

Big Crowd

Seats for the exhibition game
were quickly sold out, at $2.50
each. When Peyton Cain,
superintendent of Alpine
schools, told Mr. Herbert how
many school kids would be
disappointed to miss the game
because they couldn't afford
the steep admission price, Kokernot handed Cain 400 tickets
and told him to sell them to
his pupils for 25 cents. On
the day of the game, a mob of
autograph seekers met the Big
Leaguers when they stepped
off their train at 6:45 a.m.,
and schools and businesses
closed at noon. At game time,
a throng of more than 6,000
fans from all over the region
crammed into Kokernot Field
to witness the spectacle of
the St. Louis Browns and the
Chicago Cubs, playing major
league baseball in Alpine. Extra bleachers that stretched all
the way down both sidelines
to the outfield fences were
brought in to accommodate the
record crowd. The gathering
was the largest ever assembled
in West Texas for a single
event. All of Alpine's hotels
were booked to capacity, and
restaurants were mobbed. One
Alpine restaurant was reported
to have ordered "400 corn-fed
beef steaks" for the big day.
The *San Angelo Standard Times*
wrote, "Cowboys came up from
the Black Gap country of the
Big Bend, 'fresh-shaved' for
the first time in weeks. They
whooped every time the crack
of the bat against the ball was
heard." The public address
announcer asked the crowd,
"How many of you folks are
not residents of Alpine? Hold
up your hands." "Yiyaaa,
yipee," the crowd roared, and
at least 4,000 of the 6,000
spectators lifted hands high
into the air. Top: The west
bleachers filled to capacity.
Bottom: The east bleachers
loaded down.

Big Performance

The press box at Kokernot field was filled to capacity for the first time, and four special telegraph wires were installed so that reporters and sportswriters from Chicago, St. Louis, and New York could transmit the game back to their big city fans. Hundreds of wires and phone calls poured in from as far as Chihuahua City, where eight Mexican dignitaries tried to wrangle box seats at the last minute, regardless of the cost. During the contest, Mr. Herbert offered to pay $25 for each home run hit out of his park. He had to pay the reward three times. The Browns' American League All-Star, Al Zarilla, smashed a 350-foot homer over the right-field wall in the third inning, and Gerry Priddy, the Browns' second baseman, followed suit. Cub shortstop Ray Smalley hit a two-run homer over the left-field wall in the bottom of the fourth inning. It was a well-played game, and the throng of West Texas baseball fans got what they came for. The National League's Chicago Cubs outlasted the American League's St. Louis Browns 7–6. Exciting up to the very end, the game was the beginning of a great annual tradition of big league exhibition games at Kokernot Field. Top: Zarilla takes off after a first inning hit for the Browns. Bottom: A Cubs player is welcomed home by his teammates.

Boots and Bats

The 1949 edition of the Alpine Cowboys was the most powerful batting team that Mr. Herbert had ever assembled. During the regular season, the hard-hitting Cowboys destroyed their opponents, racking up some impressive high scores in the process. They beat the Tigua Cubs 19–0, the Conroe Wildcats 14–5, and the Randolph Field Ramblers 23–12. During the Randolph contest Cowboys Tom Jordan and Bob Baumler hit two of the longest home runs that had ever been seen at Kokernot Field. Both players sent the ball sailing over the center-field wall, 400 feet distant, clearing the wall by a good ten feet. In their first game of the Southwestern Semipro Tournament in El Paso, the Cowboys pulverized the Holloman Air Force Base club 36–0. Mr. Herbert, who routinely paid his players $100 for home runs hit in important tournaments, ended up paying Travis Cook for one homer and Baumler for two. In the second game of the tournament, the Cowboys shut out the Beaumont General Hospital club 10–0. Before the third game of the tournament against the International Oilers, which the Cowboys won 8–4, Mr. Herbert gave each of his players a pair of custom-made cowboy boots. The boots, designed and made by Tony Lama in El Paso, were red with white trim and featured a steer-head design and the words "Alpine Cowboys." Mr. Herbert (pictured front row center wearing the boots) would continue to have the custom "Alpine Cowboys" boots made for his players in the years to follow.

The Legionnaires

When Mr. Herbert began to add more and more talent to his roster, he had so many players he created a second team, originally called the Junior Cowboys. Kokernot, who was a member of the American Legion in Alpine, changed their name to the Alpine Legionnaires. Ironically, in their third game of the Southwestern Semipro Tournament in El Paso, the Cowboys ended up playing the Legionnaires for the championship. *The El Paso Times* wrote: "A capacity crowd is expected to witness the Cowboys-Legionnaires scrap which will have the unusual sidelight of both teams being sponsored by the same man, millionaire-rancher Herbert Kokernot. The Cowboys, who have won the SW title for the last two years, are favored to defeat their stable mates but the Legionnaires, composed of former Cowboys stars, will have the incentive of proving that owner Kokernot made a big mistake of discarding the players who aided him in gaining the championship." The Cowboys ended up beating their brethren 13–5, securing their third straight Southwestern Semipro Tournament championship title. In the three years the Cowboys played the El Paso tournament, they had never lost a game. After the El Paso tournament, Mr. Herbert was so impressed with the Legionnaires' performance that he picked up several of his "second team" star players to take with him and the Cowboys to the National Semipro Tournament in Wichita, including pitcher Ray Miller, catcher Larry Isbell, second baseman Jim Henry, outfielder Tommie Finger, and utility man Tom Wagner. Above: batboy Freddy Davis, who later became a federal judge in Fort Worth, wearing a Junior Cowboys uniform.

Alpine Chow Boys

Now with their third consecutive Southwestern championship wrapped up, the Cowboys turned their attention again to Wichita and the National Semi-pro Baseball Congress. Before the tournament, Mr. Herbert took his Cowboys and the Legionnaires to the 29th Paisano Baptist Encampment, where they performed serving duties on the chow line. The Paisano Camp, situated on a dramatic boulder-strewn piece of ranch land between Alpine and Marfa, had been supported by the Kokernot family for many years. Every summer, families from all over West Texas would make the pilgrimage to the annual retreat. In Wichita the Cowboys got off to a good start, pounding the Camden, Arkansas, Southern Kraftsmen 15–1 in the first game of the tournament. In their second match, the Cowboys lost to Tuscaloosa, Alabama, 4–3 and then were eliminated in their third game by the Milwaukee Falks 4–0. The Cowboys were disappointed, but they did manage to receive one distinctive honor. The National Baseball Congress selected the Alpine Cowboys as the Best Dressed Team in the tournament.

COWBOY TALES Bob Baumler, shortstop

I spent the summer of 1949 living at the Holland Hotel when Dan Blocker, "Hoss Cartwright," was at Sul Ross College. He went on to be a star of the hit television western series *Bonanza*. I have many stories and photos from that wonderful season in Alpine. I signed with the Boston Red Sox the following year.

The last time I saw Mr. Herbert was at the Waldorf Astoria, in New York City, where we had a photo taken with a Milwaukee Braves scout, and to this day I still have a handwritten letter from him.

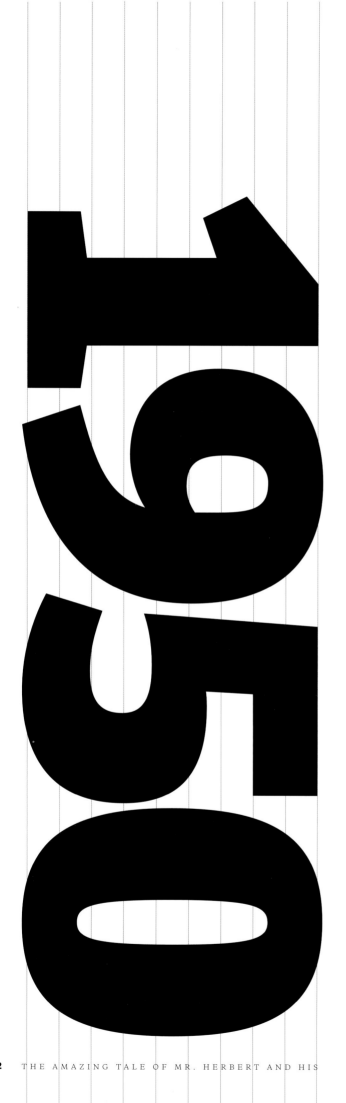

1950

Missing the Train

In March the second annual big league exhibition game was staged at Kokernot Field. A capacity crowd of 5,000 baseball fans poured into Alpine to watch the Chicago White Sox and the St. Louis Browns battle to a 5–5 tie. Once again, the big league spectacle turned out to be everything that had been touted, but the game had to be called at the end of eight and a half innings so that the two teams could catch their train. After sweeping the Southwestern Semipro Tournament in El Paso three years in a row, the Cowboys ended up missing the tournament in 1950. At the end of the 1949 season, Kokernot had told the tournament manager that the Alpine Cowboys did not want to return to El Paso because there was not enough competition in the tournament. The Cowboys changed their minds at the last minute but couldn't get into the annual meet, so they entered the Southwest National Baseball Congress Tournament in Corpus Christi instead. Pictured: A luncheon at the Holland Hotel with players and supporters.

Jolly Rancher

Chuck Devereaux (left) and Herbert Kokernot Jr. watch the 1950 edition of the Alpine Cowboys from the dugout at Kokernot Field. Devereaux, the successful freshman baseball coach at Baylor University, had been elected field captain and manager of the Cowboys prior to the season. Determined to build a winning team, Kokernot had beefed up the team's roster substantially. Nine All-Southwest Conference collegiate stars had been recruited over the off-season, and five more prominent conference performers had tentatively promised to play for the team. Mr. Herbert made his money from ranching, banking, and investments and indulged in the ball club mainly just for the fun of it. And what fun he was having by 1950. He spent large sums of money on his "hobby." The Cowboys cost Kokernot what was rumored to be more than $50,000 a year. In addition to paying his players well, Kokernot provided the boys with room and board and a generous spending allowance so that they could save all of the money they earned from baseball to pay for college expenses during the school year. "Nothing is too good for my players," he was known to say.

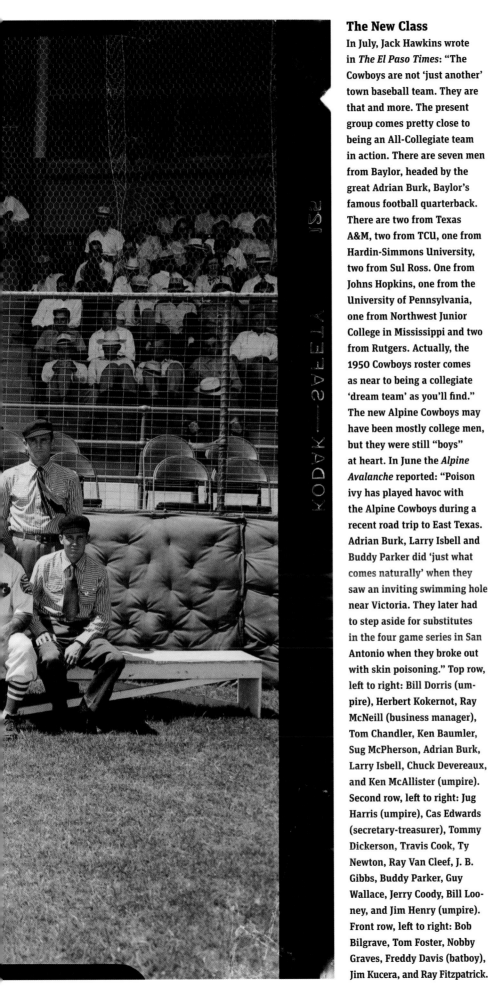

The New Class

In July, Jack Hawkins wrote in *The El Paso Times*: "The Cowboys are not 'just another' town baseball team. They are that and more. The present group comes pretty close to being an All-Collegiate team in action. There are seven men from Baylor, headed by the great Adrian Burk, Baylor's famous football quarterback. There are two from Texas A&M, two from TCU, one from Hardin-Simmons University, two from Sul Ross. One from Johns Hopkins, one from the University of Pennsylvania, one from Northwest Junior College in Mississippi and two from Rutgers. Actually, the 1950 Cowboys roster comes as near to being a collegiate 'dream team' as you'll find." The new Alpine Cowboys may have been mostly college men, but they were still "boys" at heart. In June the *Alpine Avalanche* reported: "Poison ivy has played havoc with the Alpine Cowboys during a recent road trip to East Texas. Adrian Burk, Larry Isbell and Buddy Parker did 'just what comes naturally' when they saw an inviting swimming hole near Victoria. They later had to step aside for substitutes in the four game series in San Antonio when they broke out with skin poisoning." Top row, left to right: Bill Dorris (umpire), Herbert Kokernot, Ray McNeill (business manager), Tom Chandler, Ken Baumler, Sug McPherson, Adrian Burk, Larry Isbell, Chuck Devereaux, and Ken McAllister (umpire). Second row, left to right: Jug Harris (umpire), Cas Edwards (secretary-treasurer), Tommy Dickerson, Travis Cook, Ty Newton, Ray Van Cleef, J. B. Gibbs, Buddy Parker, Guy Wallace, Jerry Coody, Bill Looney, and Jim Henry (umpire). Front row, left to right: Bob Bilgrave, Tom Foster, Nobby Graves, Freddy Davis (batboy), Jim Kucera, and Ray Fitzpatrick.

COWBOY TALES Ray Van Cleef, outfielder

My first game at Kokernot Field was quite an experience. In 1950 there was an intense rivalry between the Marfa and Alpine-area ranchers about most everything, but particularly sports competition.

That Fourth of July a game was played between the Cowboys and the Marfa Indians. Ranchers and townspeople from both areas filled the stands and the parking area along the first-base line to capacity. The Marfa folks were not to be outdone. Knowing that the Cowboys had a lineup of college and ex-professionals, they recruited former professional players and even a few who at one time played for the Cowboys. The fans, particularly the ranchers, from Marfa tried to intimidate Mr. Herbert and bet him that the Indians would win easily. Mr. Herbert and his Alpine rancher friends quickly took them up, and apparently a considerable amount of money was on the table.

Prior to the game Mr. Herbert came into the Cowboy locker room and in his shy manner said he had a special request of our team. As I recall, he said that he was not one to make speeches and never thought he would ask a special favor of his Cowboys players, but this was one time that it was important that we win the game against the Marfa team. He pointed out that his rancher friends had bet a considerable amount on us to win! With that, he said, he wanted to give us an incentive to win the game. He said that he would give $100 for a home run, $20 for a hit or a stolen base, and $100 for every run that we won by.

Now, young college players were not necessarily greedy (joke), but the temptation to win the game for Mr. Herbert plus the incentives caused our adrenalin to flow at an extremely high level! Marfa had brought in a pitcher from the Mexican league, and he put us down for several innings, without our scoring any runs. Our enthusiasm caused us to be almost out of control. But then the Marfa pitcher tired and gave up multiple hits, home runs, and stolen bases, and he even hit batsmen (some players took one for the team and the $20)! The final score was like 24-4! It turned out to be a triumphant Fourth for the Alpine folks and for Mr. Herbert.

The next day Cowboy manager Chuck Devereaux called a meeting in his Holland Hotel room. He emptied a satchel of dollar bills on the bed and announced that we all would receive equal shares of the incentive money. I recall that each of us received about $300. Not bad one-day pay for amateur college players!

Tom Terrific

Adrian Burk, the Baylor football star who had held down the first-base position for the Cowboys at the beginning of the 1950 season, left the team in July to play pro football for Baltimore. Burk, an athletic first baseman and relief pitcher, had been a mainstay for the Cowboys and was the leading hitter that year, with a big .406 batting average. He was ably replaced, however, by Tom Chandler of Dallas, a 1948 Baylor graduate who had made the All-Southwest Conference team for three years. It was the beginning of a long and influential partnership between Chandler, Kokernot, and the Alpine Cowboys. Chandler started contributing immediately. In the ninth inning of a crucial Southwest NBC tournament game in Corpus Christi, he brought the Cowboys from behind with a dramatic 370-foot homer over the left-field fence to deliver a 6–5 win over the powerful Sinton Plymouth Oilers. The victory helped to propel the Cowboys into the final playoff series against the Weimar Truckers. In the second game against Weimar for the Texas State Semi-pro baseball title, Weimar had gone ahead 15–11 in the top of the eighth inning. Tom Chandler led off the bottom of the ninth with a one-run home run. The Cowboys then batted around, and Chandler came up again. This time, with the bases loaded, he hit a double and the Cowboys won the championship 16–15. The celebration (pictured) followed. The Cowboys went on to win fourth place in the National Semipro meet at Wichita.

In Full Stride

When the 1951 edition of the Alpine Cowboys took the field again, they were stronger than ever and feeling confident. The previous year had been the Cowboys' best showing yet. They had won the Texas Semipro title and were fourth in the national meet at Wichita, Kansas. They had never lost a game in Texas and Southwestern tournament play in their four years as an organization. They had swept the Southwestern Semipro tournament in El Paso three years in a row, but in 1950, through a realignment of districts, they ended up playing in the National Baseball Congress Semipro tournament, played in Corpus Christi. The Cowboys

wanted badly to return to the El Paso tournament in the coming year, but the commissioner for the National Baseball Congress would not release the Cowboys from his jurisdiction so that they could do so. Regardless of that ruling, the Cowboys charged ahead at full throttle. Mr. Herbert had continued to sweeten the roster, so by the start of the new season, he had more than 40 college boys on his 06 Ranch payrolls playing for the Cowboys or the Junior Cowboys. Pictured: Baylor star Jerry Coody, who landed the shortstop position at the beginning of the season.

Herbert's Day

In early July 1951, baseball fans from all over West Texas paid tribute to Mr. Herbert with a special Herbert L. Kokernot Baseball Day in Alpine. Stores and businesses closed, and a parade led by the Alpine High School Band wound its way from downtown to Kokernot Field, where a throng of well-wishers had gathered to honor "the nation's foremost baseball fan." During the opening ceremonies, local sportscaster Marvin Kay gave a personal introduction of Mr. Herbert and each of the Cowboys players, and Alpine mayor John Gillette and County Judge Felix McGaughey read official proclamations that established the special day. District Judge Alan Fraser presented Kokernot a bronze plaque with these words engraved on it: "Herbert Kokernot Baseball Day, Alpine, Texas, July 7, 1951. Presented to Herbert Kokernot as evidence of the appreciation of the people of Alpine for his community service and as a reminder of his hometown's continued good wishes and thanks." Then Mr. Herbert tossed out the first ball for a game between his beloved Alpine Cowboys and the Conroe Wildcats. Pictured top row, left to right: Larry Isbell, Milton Isenberg, Nobby Graves, Bruce Falk, Dan Watson, Jim Shamblin, Lloyd Jenny, and John Boone. Bottom row, left to right: Herbert Kokernot, Chuck Devereaux (manager), Roger Johnson, Ty Newton, Ray Van Cleef, Tom Chandler, Jerry Coody, and Cas Edwards (secretary-treasurer). Batboy: Freddy Davis.

COWBOY TALES Ty Newton, second baseman

Jim Shamblin, our third baseman, decided to leave the team and go back to Houston for some reason. They took up a collection in the stands on a Sunday afternoon, and he got a nice send-off. The next week he returned to the lineup and continued the year with us.

One of my fun experiences was getting to fly frequently with J. O. Casparis. He was hired by the ranchers to shoot coyotes that were killing their cattle. He had a small single-engine plane with the door taken off on the left side. He would fly with a shotgun across his lap, and when he spotted a coyote he would dive down, lean out the side, and shoot. I don't recall seeing him miss. I had always been interested in flying, and that was a great adventure for me. As it turned out, I was called into the Air Force, went into pilot training, and spent 30 years as a career pilot.

As an 18-year-old boy who had just finished my freshman year on a baseball scholarship at Baylor, I felt that I was the most fortunate kid in the world to have been involved with the Alpine Cowboys. Mr. Kokernot was one of the most generous people I have known, and he loved baseball and loved helping college kids.

I played the summers of 1950, 1951, part of 1952, and 1954. In 1953 I had signed with the Chicago Cubs and was playing Class A ball in the South Atlantic League. In 1954 I received my contract from the Cubs and, shortly after, received a letter from Uncle Sam to enter the Air Force. That meant that I had to go to summer camp in 1954. After finishing camp, my wife and I went to Alpine for the last month of the season. During my years at Alpine, we lived free in the Holland Hotel, ate any place in town, and just signed the ticket, and Mr. Kokernot paid for it. We were treated like celebrities by the people in town.

Mr. Herbert, as he was called, had special days when he paid for hits, runs, and home runs, and the money was split among the players. We had a ballpark that was as good as any in the country, and better than most, including minor league parks. When we traveled, we traveled first class, sometimes flying by chartered plane and staying in the best hotels.

We were fortunate to win the State Semipro Championship three times and play in the National Semipro tournament in Wichita, Kansas. Along the way we got to play against many major league ball players, some of whom were drafted during the Korean War and were playing for Army teams at Fort Bliss and Fort Sam Houston. We also got to participate in roundups and chuck-wagon dinners at Mr. Herbert's ranch. Being part of the Alpine Cowboys is an experience that I have cherished and relayed to others many times over the years. I will always be thankful for the opportunity.

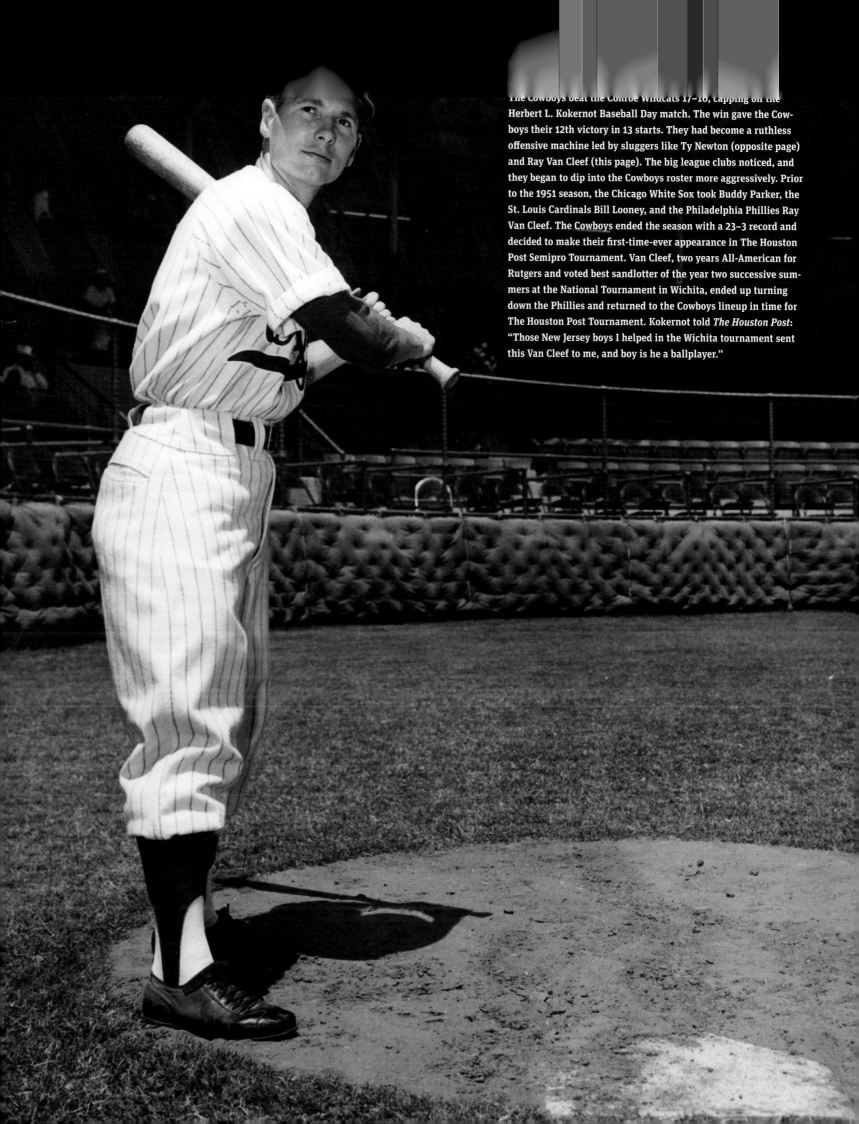

The Cowboys beat the Conroe Whitcats 17–16, capping off the Herbert L. Kokernot Baseball Day match. The win gave the Cowboys their 12th victory in 13 starts. They had become a ruthless offensive machine led by sluggers like Ty Newton (opposite page) and Ray Van Cleef (this page). The big league clubs noticed, and they began to dip into the Cowboys roster more aggressively. Prior to the 1951 season, the Chicago White Sox took Buddy Parker, the St. Louis Cardinals Bill Looney, and the Philadelphia Phillies Ray Van Cleef. The Cowboys ended the season with a 23–3 record and decided to make their first-time-ever appearance in The Houston Post Semipro Tournament. Van Cleef, two years All-American for Rutgers and voted best sandlotter of the year two successive summers at the National Tournament in Wichita, ended up turning down the Phillies and returned to the Cowboys lineup in time for The Houston Post Tournament. Kokernot told *The Houston Post*: "Those New Jersey boys I helped in the Wichita tournament sent this Van Cleef to me, and boy is he a ballplayer."

Paper Boys

In August Mr. Herbert checked the team into the Buccaneer Hotel in Galveston for The Houston Post Tournament. Clark Nealon wrote in *The Houston Post*: "Managed by Chuck Devereaux, Baylor's freshman baseball coach, the Cowboys are known far and wide as the 'best dressed team' in semipro baseball, and their wealthy sponsor has presented each player with fancy cowboy boots—done in the team's colors of red and white—for off the diamond wear. Fabulous is the word for the Cowboys." Larry Isbell (this page) and Jim Shamblin (opposite page) posed for *The Houston Post* photographers, and the rest of the team were treated like baseball celebrities when they arrived at the big city tournament. The Cowboys were the clear favorites going into their first game, but they were upset by the Shell Oilers of Houston 6–4 in front of 1,438 fans at Buffalo Stadium. The Oilers scored four unearned runs in the third inning, as shortstop Guy Wallace made three errors, and then added their two decisive runs in the fifth inning on three hits and an error by Jim Shamblin at third base. Van Cleef got three hits, including a double, and Wallace got two singles. Nobby Graves pitched a good game, but the loose defensive play did the team in.

Good Guys

The Cowboys bounced back decisively in their second game of The Houston Post Tournament, beating the Kemah Laundry Sea Gulls 11–1. Guy Wallace (opposite page) redeemed himself with some strong defensive plays, and John Boone (this page), the former University of Houston standout, hurled five innings of no-hit baseball. Van Cleef and Tom Chandler led the scoring barrage for the Cowboys.

High Flyers

Before the Cowboys' third game of The Houston Post Tournament against the Baytown Humble Oilers, Mr. Herbert promised the boys that he would move them from Galveston to the luxurious Shamrock Hotel in Houston if they won the game. The bribe worked. The Cowboys walloped the Oilers 10–0, and the team moved into the Shamrock. In the fourth game, the Cowboys easily handled the Richmond Tigers 11–0 and then beat the Victoria Rosebuds 8–5, setting Alpine up for a final game against the Columbus Redbirds. A flurry of telegrams from fans and supporters cheering the boys on poured into the Shamrock Hotel before the big game, but in the end the Cowboys lost the game 2–5 and were the runners-up in the tournament. Mr. Herbert was so pleased with the team's performance, he packed up the boys and flew them to Colorado for a little rest and relaxation. Top row, left to right: Ray Fitzpatrick, pilot, Jim Kucera, Ty Newton, Bob Bilgraves, Ken Baumler, Jerry Coody, Tom Foster, Sug McPherson, Chuck Devereaux, and Nobby Graves. Bottom row, left to right: Marvin Kay, Buddy Parker, Bill Looney, Guy Wallace, Travis Cook, Ray Van Cleef, Tom Chandler, Herbert Kokernot, and Larry Isbell. Batboy: Freddy Davis.

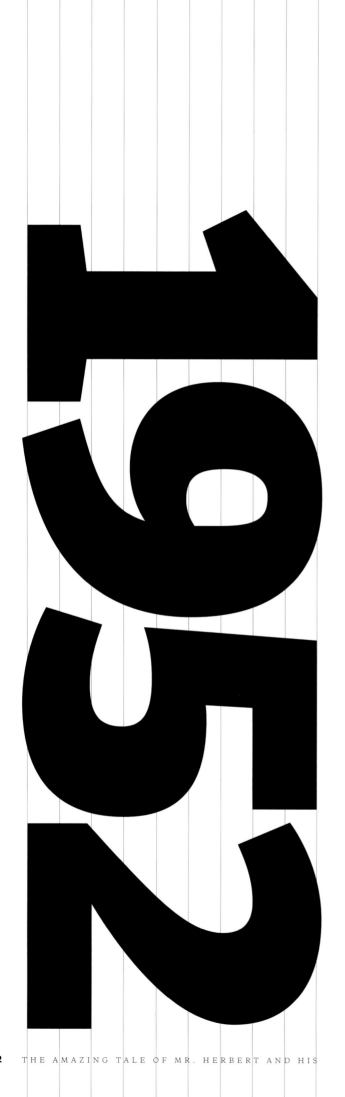

1952

Back Home

Tom Chandler, coaching from the third-base line, sends Larry Isbell home in a game against the Sandia AFB Bombers. At the beginning of the season, Mr. Herbert had elevated Chandler to team manager. Chandler had been an All-Conference player at Baylor two years in a row and had led the Southwest Conference in home runs in 1947. He had played a major role in the Cowboys' successful 28-and-5 run the year before and was instrumental in the team's second place showing at The Houston Post National Tournament. Chandler was a natural leader and popular with the players. During his first two years as a Cowboy, he had become an important confidant of Mr. Herbert, who relied on him for his baseball knowledge and savvy recruitment advice. Now in his third year as a Cowboy, Chandler began his long and influential player-manager role with the ball club.

El Paso–Alpine Cowboys

In early June the Cowboys got off to a good start, walloping the Grandfalls Eagles 13–1 in their season opener, and then headed to El Paso for a three-game stand with the powerful Fort Bliss Falcons. But in El Paso, the Cowboys ran into trouble, losing all three games to the soldier nine. After the crushing defeat, Mr. Herbert announced that he was planning to completely rebuild his team. In June, when Kokernot sent in his application to enter the Southwestern Tournament in El Paso, he conspicuously left off the team's roster. After missing the tournament the past two years in a row, he was determined to get into the tourney this time around. The Cowboys were accepted into the regional series, but they had to enter as an El Paso team in order to avoid a jurisdictional dispute with the San Antonio Tournament. The team had fulfilled the requirements for such a maneuver by playing the Fort Bliss series. Now they were officially known as the El Paso–Alpine Cowboys for the remainder of the season. Kokernot and Chandler began making improvements to the roster in preparation for the Southwestern tournament. Top row, left to right: Allen Thomas (umpire), Herbert Kokernot, Ty Newton, Bob Moore, Ronnie Harrison, Bill McClaren, Jug Harris, Chuck Ellis, Bill Looney, Cas Edwards, and W. J. Edens (umpire). Bottom row, left to right: Dick Sutter, Tom Chandler, Joe Youngblood, Chick Zomlefer, Doyle Stout, Sonny Bollman, Ed Kneupper, Arthur Blair, and Lloyd Moore. Batboy: Joe Don Looney.

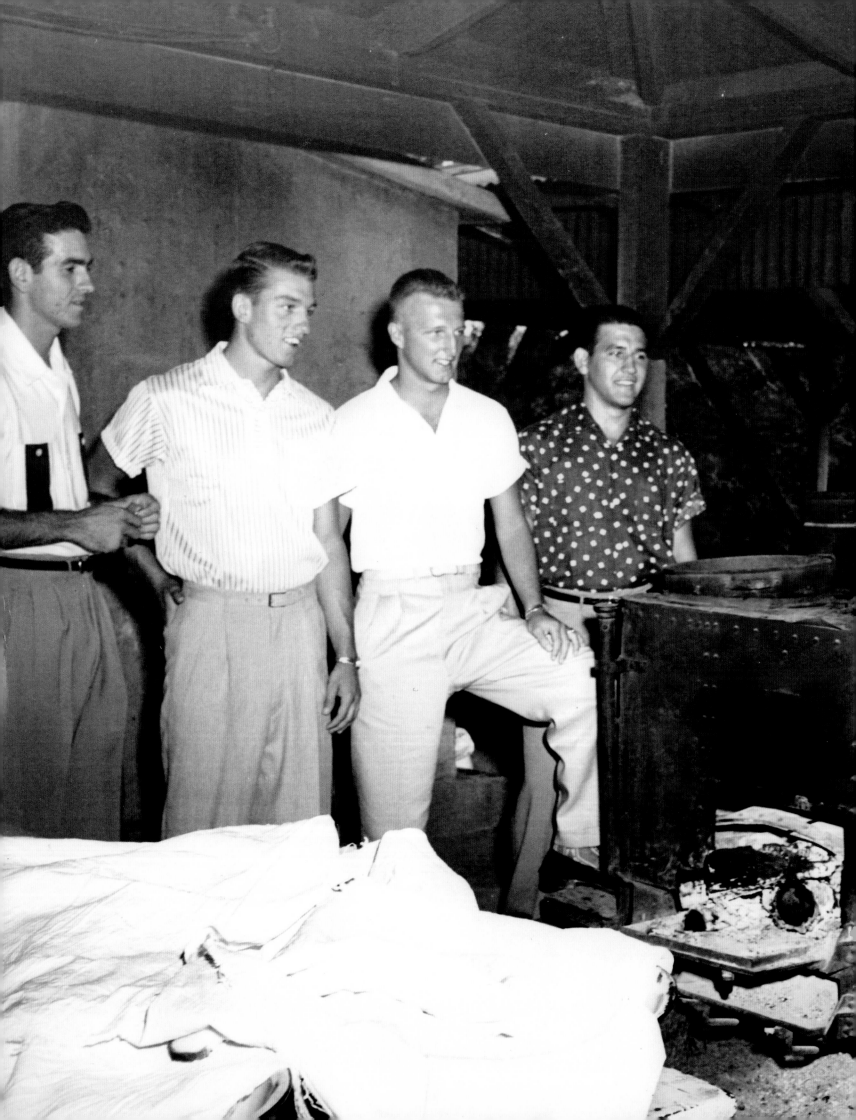

Dallas Cowboys

Toward the end of June the Cowboys got back to their winning ways. They beat the Tony Lama Cowboys 7–3 and then had a chance to avenge their previous three losses to the Fort Bliss Falcons in a two-game rematch. Before the first game, Mr. Herbert came into the locker room and offered the boys $100 each if they beat the Falcons and $25 every time they got on base. The Cowboys redeemed themselves by winning the grudge match 8–4, and Kokernot handed over the money. In early July the Cowboys beat the Jal Gassers 4–2. The winning pitcher in the game was an 18-year-old high school star from Dallas named Doyle Stout (second from left). In the game against the Jal Gassers, Stout went all the way on the mound to get the win. Chandler told Louis Cox in the *Dallas Times Herald* that the Cowboys were younger than ever, explaining: "In the past we've taken the cream of the College players. Mr. Kokernot found it pretty hard to compete with the service teams, so he decided this year to pick up the leading high school players and combine them with a few of the best college players, building up a team for the future." Tommy Bowers (far right) was also from Dallas, where he had been a sensational All-Southwest Conference hurler for SMU. Both pitchers had been brought in by Chandler to strengthen the Cowboys lineup going into the Southwestern Semipro Tournament.

Missile Defense

In July the heavily fortified "tournament team" of the Alpine Cowboys (pictured) entered the Southwestern Semipro Tournament in El Paso. The Cowboys beat the Guided Missiles of Fort Bliss in the first contest 2–0 and then galloped into the winners' bracket finals by blasting the defending champion Tony Lama Cowboys 11–2. That set up a grudge match between the Cowboys and their old nemesis, the Fort Bliss Falcons. The Cowboys ended up with a surprisingly easy victory, beating the Falcons 13–4, which sent them into the tourney finals. Remarkably, the Cowboys had still never lost a game in the four years that they had participated in the Southwestern Semipro Tournament. But in a second match against Fort Bliss in the finals, the Cowboys were handed their first loss ever in the annual El Paso tournament, losing to the Falcons 7–5. That set up a final championship game with the pesky Fort Bliss team. The highly anticipated game started out as a seesaw affair, but a grand slam by Ronnie Harrison in the fourth inning did the trick for the Cowboys, giving them a final 8–3 victory and their fourth Southwestern Semipro Tournament championship in as many appearances. The Cowboys then went on to beat the Sandia AFB Bombers of New Mexico, the winner of the Northern division of the Southwestern tournament, in a championship series back in Alpine, which made the Cowboys the undisputed Southwestern champs and qualified them for the National Baseball Congress Tournament in Wichita. Pictured, players top row, left to right: Bill McClaren, Lou Berberet, Chuck Ellis, Pete Swain, Jim Fiscalini, Ed Kneupper, Jug Harris, and Ty Newton. Bottom row, left to right: Tom Chandler, Ronnie Harrison, Doyle Stout, Chick Zomlefer, Sonny Bollman, Lloyd Moore, Arthur Blair, Ivan Abromowitz, and Tommy Bowers.

COWBOY TALES Pete Swain, outfielder

My first exposure to the Alpine Cowboys, Mr. Herbert, Tom Chandler, and the good people of Alpine was in 1952. I was in the Army at El Paso and playing baseball for the Fort Bliss Falcons. We played the Cowboys in the play-off game to see which team would represent the district in the national NBC tournament at Wichita, Kansas. Alpine won the game, and Mr. Herbert picked up four of us to go to Wichita with them. The lucky four consisted of Lou Berberet, Ivan Abromowitz, Jim Fiscalini, and me. We drove from Fort Bliss to Alpine and worked out for two days at Kokernot Field. Mr. Herbert chartered a plane and flew us, many of the town folks, and the radio announcer to Wichita and put everyone up at the Broadmore Hotel. I am sorry to say we didn't win the tournament, but we were duly impressed. From the barracks to the Broadmore Hotel.

It was always a pleasure to play at the "House Mr. Herbert Built." The field was manicured perfectly and always in great shape. Mr. Herbert had a gentleman, Pedro, who did nothing but work on the field the year-round. He, too, loved baseball and took great pride in "his" baseball field. I know Mr. Herbert was very proud of the Cowboys and the stadium he had built.

Switch Hitters
The hard-hitting Fort Bliss star Pete Swain (opposite page) had been a major contributor to the Cowboys' four losses to the Falcons in the regular season of 1952, and he had been a major headache for Mr. Herbert and his team when he played against the Cowboys in the Southwestern Semipro tourney. Kokernot, taking the philosophy that if you can't beat 'em, join 'em, asked Swain to switch sides at the end of the Southwestern championship series to play for the Cowboys in the National Semipro Baseball Congress tournament in Wichita. Johnny Creel (this page) also joined the Cowboys just for the National tournament. He had been playing professional ball with the Dallas Eagles during the regular season.

Hats Off to Herbert

The 1953 season kicked off with the fifth annual big league exhibition game, featuring the Chicago Cubs and the St. Louis Browns. More than 2,000 baseball fans from all over the Southwest turned out to see the Browns beat the Cubs 9–4 and to watch baseball legend Satchel Paige pitch for the Browns. Following the game Mr. Herbert hosted a big barbecue at the O6 Ranch, where he presented the managers of the two major league clubs Kokernot-style Stetsons. Shortly afterward Mr. Herbert was part of another presentation. The National Baseball Congress designated Herbert Kokernot the "Sponsor of the Decade."

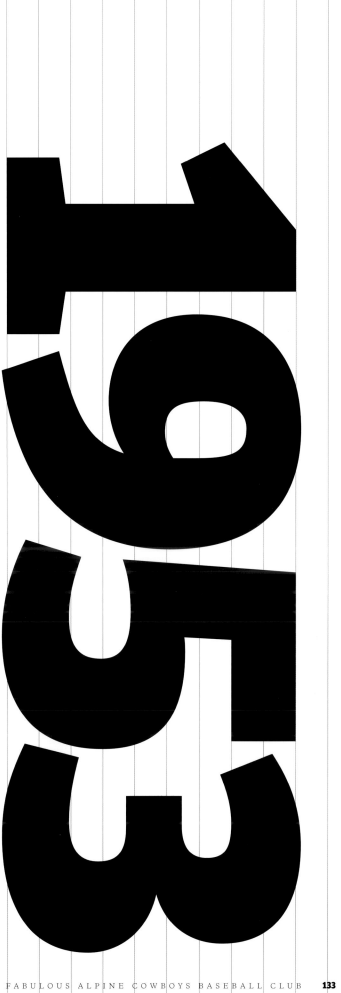

The Class of '53

The Cowboys won the first four games of the regular season. Many of the new players on the squad were either college boys or high school graduates. High school standouts joining the team included outfielder and pitcher James Skinner, an all-state basketball player from Irving High School; left-handed pitcher Doyle Stout, from Crozier Tech High School in Dallas; shortstop Doyle Traylor, an all-state football star from Temple High School; and outfielder Jerry Mallett, from Beaumont High School. New college recruits included third baseman Johnny Carruthers, an all-conference SMU player who had been the second leading hitter in the Southwest conference the past season; pitcher Tommy Bowers, who was also an all-conference star at SMU; and first baseman and outfielder Tommy Snow, an all-conference player from The University of Texas. Pitcher Boyd Linker, a former star of the NCAA collegiate series, and second-baseman Buddy Stevenson, an all-conference standout, were also newcomers from The University of Texas. Slim Henson and first baseman Norman Cash had recently transferred from San Angelo College. Pictured, top row, left to right: Tommy Bowers, Doyle Stout, Buddy Stephenson, James Skinner, and Johnny Carruthers. Bottom row, left to right: Tommy Snow, Tom Chandler, Doyle Traylor, and Carroll Simpson.

COWBOY TALES Tommy Snow, outfielder

It was the summer of 1953. Boyd Linker and I had just arrived in Alpine after competing in the College World Series in Omaha for the Longhorns. We were both sophomores at UT. We lost in the championship game to Michigan 7-5.

Tom Chandler had invited us both to come to Alpine and play for the Cowboys that summer. All we had seen of Alpine was from the rear of the train we rode from Austin to Tucson, Arizona, for the play-off (two out of three) to see who would represent District 6 in Omaha that year. As the train slowly proceeded through Alpine, we went out on the rear of the last car and watched to get an idea of what it would be like to spend the summer there. We knew at the time we would be coming back. It was in the middle of the famous 50s drought. From the back of the train the town was really not too impressive.

When we did get to Alpine, our dorm room on the Sul Ross campus was not ready, so Tom Chandler arranged a room for us at the Holland Hotel. It was a room with one bed, no curtains, and a stained white shade over the large window (remember, no air-conditioning then) facing the street. We opened the window and pulled down the shade as we prepared for a good night's sleep. After we had been asleep for a short time, an ear-bursting noise erupted that caused us both to bolt upright in bed simultaneously. The hotel began to shake. A bright white light illuminated the window shade. The roar got louder and louder. At this point we were convinced it was an earthquake or a ship from Mars. When we finally concluded it was a train, we were convinced it was off the track and about to enter into the hotel and specifically our room. Our hearts were pounding. We may have recited a few prayers. Well, of course, when the engine proceeded past the hotel, the noise began to subside, and we decided the train was still on the track. After some time, the train finally passed through and everything settled down. However, that was not the last time that night a freight train came through town. We didn't get much sleep, but at least we did not have a stroke each time one passed.

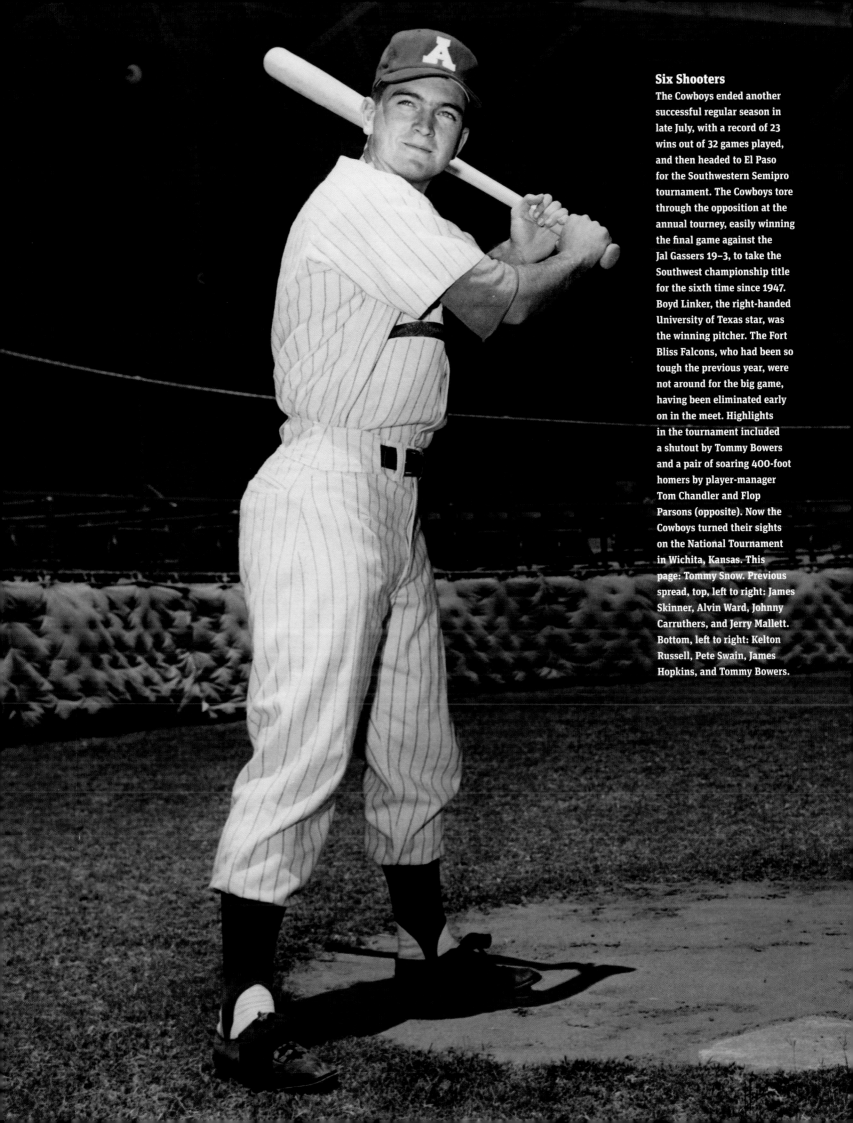

Six Shooters

The Cowboys ended another successful regular season in late July, with a record of 23 wins out of 32 games played, and then headed to El Paso for the Southwestern Semipro tournament. The Cowboys tore through the opposition at the annual tourney, easily winning the final game against the Jal Gassers 19–3, to take the Southwest championship title for the sixth time since 1947. Boyd Linker, the right-handed University of Texas star, was the winning pitcher. The Fort Bliss Falcons, who had been so tough the previous year, were not around for the big game, having been eliminated early on in the meet. Highlights in the tournament included a shutout by Tommy Bowers and a pair of soaring 400-foot homers by player-manager Tom Chandler and Flop Parsons (opposite). Now the Cowboys turned their sights on the National Tournament in Wichita, Kansas. This page: Tommy Snow. Previous spread, top, left to right: James Skinner, Alvin Ward, Johnny Carruthers, and Jerry Mallett. Bottom, left to right: Kelton Russell, Pete Swain, James Hopkins, and Tommy Bowers.

Life Lessons

Stars of the 1953 Alpine Cowboys, including my dad, Doyle Stout, second from left, get some pointers from manager Tom Chandler. Chandler was an iconic and popular leader for the team for many years and an influential figure in my father's life. He was from Dallas, like my dad and the other players pictured here, and he was a strong advocate for my father's joining the Cowboys. Chandler was at the Texas State High School Championship game in Austin with Herbert Kokernot when my dad broke the Texas high school strikeout record. After that game, Chandler and Kokernot met with my dad and invited him to come play for the Cowboys in Alpine. That is how my father was able to go to college, where he eventually earned his master's degree. All of the players pictured here were also students at Sul Ross college at the time. Left to right: Leo Burkhalter (first baseman), Doyle Stout (pitcher), Howard Snodgrass (third baseman), Clifford "Red" Jones (pitcher), R. L. Patterson (catcher), Tom Chandler (manager/first baseman), Larry Cummings (outfielder/first baseman), and Tommy Bowers (pitcher).

COWBOY TALES Doyle Stout, pitcher

After the final game of the 1952 Texas High School State Championship in Austin, I accepted Tom Chandler and Herbert Kokernot's invitation to join the Alpine Cowboys, and it was not a bad choice.

I traveled home from Austin, spent one day, and departed for the unknown, the mystical Alpine, Texas. My parents didn't object, didn't approve, didn't offer to discuss the item, so I packed my bag and the following day caught a ride with Coach Charles Stubblefield, who himself was on the way to play summer baseball in a Class D league in the West Texas–New Mexico area. Unknown to me but welcome were two more of our best players from Crozier Tech, Jesse Parades and R. L. Patterson. I think Coach Stubblefield made a deal with Tom Chandler and said, "Give them a try." Together we traveled with our wonderful Coach from built-up areas in the Dallas area to wide-open spaces that were certainly less inhabited, and, folks, it was a long, long drive. In my young life, I had made only one trip, and that was to San Antonio with my parents. West Texas took on a look that I had never imagined, and I kept thinking we were lost. But the wise old Coach Stubblefield knew better and just continued the push, reliving the games, the missed plays and opportunities, the glory of unexpected good luck and heart-winning efforts by the Cinderella team. Once in a while we would stop and sometimes have another hot dog or hamburger, another Coke, and away we would go again—to eternity or the end of the world, I was sure, perhaps another name for Alpine and Brewster County.

In those days traveling by automobile was not fast. The roads were mostly two lanes, with people passing each other in opposite directions at about 60 mph, no really good headlamps, and the common factor that everyone was tired from traveling for too many hours. Being 18 years old, though, I was adept at catching a quick nap. I'd look around at the scenery that seemed to be going from good to bad and then into the drought area of West Texas, with tumbleweeds that I had never seen before, dust storms, no rain, and once in a great while a small village or town with old automobiles and older-looking people, not modern at all. I was beginning to have real misgivings about Valhalla and Alpine.

Eventually the flat world of West Texas starting to rise, a few foothills could be seen, and even some greenery revealed itself in the distance. We were going into foothills, and in the far distance I could see larger hills, perhaps mountains, but something was all of a sudden looking a lot better. At 30 miles away, if you know how you can see great distances in West Texas, Coach Stubblefield proudly said, "That is Alpine." He finally had my attention, as we could see a place that looked nicer, with trees, greenery, an antelope—the first one for me—lots of cows, and hills and mountains. After a great while, I could see a few cars, a few houses, and a small town, and it was indeed small, when all that I had known for 18 years was Dallas County, with its heavy traffic and pickup trucks.

After a few how y'alls, we found a room in one of the local motels, had dinner, and got a good night's sleep. Sightseeing of the city we did not do, but I soon realized that would have taken only another ten minutes, plus the ballpark was not lighted, so we would not have been able to see it anyhow. The next day, we met Tom Chandler at Kokernot Field, and I was knocked off my feet and even today still remember the strong feeling of a wonderful dream and what is this all about? It was the beginning of a great adventure for me and one that changed my life and my perceptions and provided me a chance that a poor boy would not have had except for the gift of baseball, the good Lord's blessings, and an opportunity that I stepped out to grab—and it was a good decision, indeed, a major one for me.

Dog Days

In late August the Cowboys cruised to an opening game victory in the National Semipro Baseball Tournament at Wichita, beating the Laramie, Wyoming, champions 16–0. Once again Cowboys pitcher Boyd Linker (this page), who had started the season slowly, really came on strong in the tournament. In the Laramie game he registered 14 strikeouts, hit a homer, and was credited with three RBIs. Former Fort Bliss star Pete Swain hit a home run, a double, and a single and got three RBIs. Catcher Tony DiPrimio (opposite page) hit a pair of doubles. The game was halted in the sixth inning because of the tournament's ten-run rule. The Cowboys looked like they could go all the way, but in their second match they ended up losing to the tough San Diego Marine Devil Dogs 3–0. Boyd Linker pitched his second tournament shutout against the New Carlisle, Ohio, Fords in the third game, paving the way for an 8–0 Cowboys win. In the fourth game against the Springfield, Massachusetts, Westinghouse Electrics the Cowboys committed eight errors and were eliminated from the tournament. The summer was over.

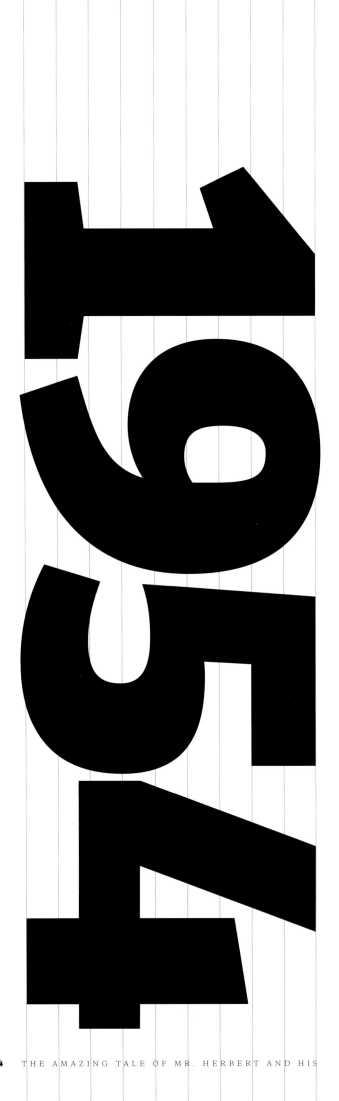

1954

THE AMAZING TALE OF MR. HERBERT AND HIS

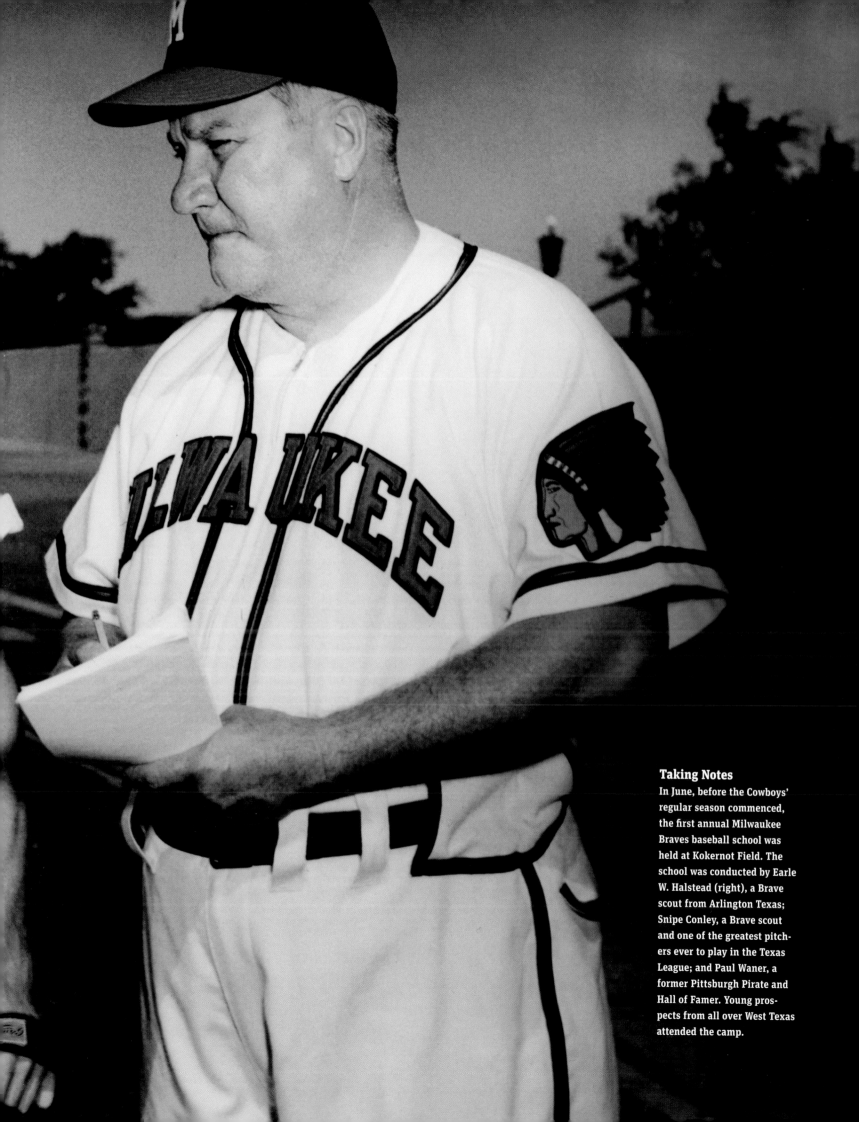

Taking Notes

In June, before the Cowboys' regular season commenced, the first annual Milwaukee Braves baseball school was held at Kokernot Field. The school was conducted by Earle W. Halstead (right), a Brave scout from Arlington Texas; Snipe Conley, a Brave scout and one of the greatest pitchers ever to play in the Texas League; and Paul Waner, a former Pittsburgh Pirate and Hall of Famer. Young prospects from all over West Texas attended the camp.

Hall Pass

Paul Waner, known as "Big Poison" while playing for the Pittsburgh Pirates, and the last player in the major leagues to get 3,000 hits in his career, conducted a batting demonstration for the attendees of the Milwaukee Braves baseball school at Kokernot Field (left). The inaugural event attracted boys from Alpine, Boerne, Sanderson, Sonora, Odessa, Sweetwater, Monahans, Fort Stockton, Valentine, Mason, Big Lake, Del Rio, Seguin, Dallas, and Houston. Following the workshop, the Milwaukee Braves baseball school All-Stars and the Alpine Cowboys played two exhibition games. After school the instructors, Cowboys players, and other local VIPs were guests of Mr. Herbert at a barbecue supper at the Alpine Legion Hall. During the event, Paul Waner, Herbert Kokernot, and Earle Halstead met longtime Alpine resident John W. Sutton, who at the time was the oldest living big league player, at 93 years old. Sutton, born in 1860, played his first major league game with the St. Louis Cardinals in 1879 and played with the New York Yankees in 1881.

COWBOY TALES Willowdean Chandler, wife

Back when they had Braves tryout schools in Alpine, Paul Waner, a very famous infielder and hitter, came to Sul Ross to help. He told Tom Chandler that there was a boy in high school down in North Carolina who is going to be a great pitcher. He had seen him with his own eyes. So, Tom contacted the boy's father, hoping to recruit the boy to pitch for the Cowboys, but was turned down. The boy hadn't passed his English class and therefore wasn't able to graduate. Tom finally talked the father into allowing the boy to play, as long as he took a correspondence English class from Texas Tech University. So when the dad brought the boy down to Alpine, he carried with him an old cardboard suitcase, tied with a rope, and a box. The box was brimming with dried tobacco leaves, for all the boys.

Come practice time, the boy was afraid to throw too hard because he was worried that he might hit someone. That boy could pitch better than anyone they had seen but, boy, was he wild. Tom would coach him, "Just throw to the mitt."

I was his teacher for the correspondence class, and we had a workbook. The first lesson wasn't great, and it didn't get any better. So I ended up answering all the questions for him. Through the season, I would get his assignments, fill in the answers, and send them in. I didn't answer all of them correctly. It came time for him to take his exam. This was to be done in front of a principal. We didn't know how he was going to make it through. Then we remembered that Chuck Ellis was the principal of Marathon High School. So there we sat, Chuck and his wife, Tom, and I, in the car on the road to a game, taking his exam for him. And that is the story of Gaylord Perry.

No Tourney

Before the start of the 1954 season, Mr. Herbert announced that he did not expect to enter the Cowboys in any tournaments that year—"unless," he said, "I decide to hold one of my own here." The Cowboys had been shifted into the Texas district, which made them ineligible for the Southwestern Semipro Tournament in El Paso that they had dominated over the years. Instead, Kokernot put the team on a challenging regular season schedule. The Cowboys started the year with a pair of games with one of the state's toughest semipro ball clubs, the Plymouth Sinton Oilers. The Cowboys jumped on the Oilers in the first game, winning the contest 11–2. Newcomer Leo Burkhalter contributed a single, double, and triple to the Cowboys' effort. But in the second match Sinton turned the tables, clouting the error-prone Cowboys 16–0.

Big D Boys

In early June, Tom Chandler returned for his sixth season as player-manager of the Alpine Cowboys and was assisted that year by his two veterans, Pete Swain and Chuck Ellis. Prior to the 1954 season, Chandler had recruited two young prospects from his Adamson High School squad in Dallas, pitcher Clifford "Red" Jones (this page), who had recently made the all-tournament team at the Texas State Championship series, and first baseman Leo Burkhalter (opposite page), who had been named utility player on the state all-star team. Larry Cummings, an all-district first baseman from Kilgore High School, was also brought on board. All three of the high school boys enrolled at Sul Ross college on Mr. Herbert's nickel. The Cowboys' young pitching ace, Tommy Bowers of SMU, returned as well, but right-hander Boyd Linker, who had performed so well for the Cowboys at the end of the previous season, did not return. He had been lured away to the rival Plymouth Sinton Oilers.

The Cowboys had a respectable year given the challenging schedule they had embarked upon. In 30 games played, the Cowboys won 19, lost ten and tied one. They scored a total of 204 runs while their opponents scored 150. Since starting play in 1946, the Cowboys had played 278 games, won 209, lost 68, scored a total of 2,376 runs to their opponents' 1,308. The 1954 team, made up mostly of Sul Ross college students, was supported by a few mainstay veterans. Pete Swain (this page), a knowledgeable seasoned player, had become an influential leader for the team. He led the Cowboys' hitting for the second year in a row, with a .452 batting average, before injuring his leg in a game at Durango, Colorado. Another veteran player, Flop Parsons, ended the season with 35 hits, three home runs, and 20 RBIs. Experienced Jimmy Hopkins (opposite page), with 79 at-bats, led the team with 22 RBIs. Former Cowboy star Ray Van Cleef, who returned to the team in July after a two-year absence, was a big midseason boost for the young ball club, ending the year with a respectable .319 batting average.

Sitting One Out

On a Sunday in July a large enthusiastic crowd packed into Kokernot Field for a double-header with the Refugio Vets and to show their appreciation for Mr. Herbert and his Alpine Cowboys. The day was officially proclaimed "Baseball Appreciation Day" in Alpine. At the opening ceremonies, Mayor Hugh White read an official proclamation and introduced the players. The *Alpine Avalanche* reported on the event: "The occasion was a great success, the only sour note in the whole affair being the Cowboys' inability to hand their sponsor a victory. But Mr. Kokernot took the loss in stride, remarking, 'Well, we can't win 'em all.'" With no tournaments in their plans the Cowboys took a swing through Colorado for their final series of the season. When they returned to Alpine Mr. Herbert hosted the team and their wives and dates at a farewell dinner, where he again awarded custom red and white Alpine Cowboys boots to the players. Back row, left to right: Leo Burkhalter, Doyle Stout, Howard Snodgrass, Ty Newton, James Thomas, Tommy Bowers, Jim Hopkins, Chuck Ellis, Kelton Russell, Red Jones, Buddy Watts, and Jim Spradley. Front row, left to right: Norman Cash, Duane "Flop" Parsons, R. L. Patterson, Tom Chandler, Herbert Kokernot, Cas Edwards, Alvin Ward, Jim Bell, Roy Lewis, and Ray Van Cleef. Batboys, left to right: Dale Hoffman and Bain Ward.

COWBOY TALES Red Jones, pitcher

I knew Tom Chandler as a high school coach. I was a fastball pitcher, and Tom didn't want me throwing curve balls, so he taught me how to throw a slider, which was easier on the arm. Tom had a great sense of humor. When people would ask him how his struggling team was doing, he would say: "You win a few, you lose a few, and you have a few rained out. We are not winning, and it's not raining."

When he had a dispute with an umpire, he would turn his cap bill sideways and get in the ump's face. Wearing your cap sideways is not a new thing, as you may have thought. Tom started it.

Hale Mary

Tom Chandler looks on as movie actor Monte Hale lobs the ceremonial first ball high into the air to start the Alpine Cowboys' ninth semipro season. Hale had been in Marfa at the time with Elizabeth Taylor, Rock Hudson, and James Dean, filming *Giant*, the epic Texas movie about the mythic King Ranch, which in reality is located in South Texas. Mr. Herbert had invited Hale to toss out the first ball of a doubleheader with the powerful Jal Gassers at Kokernot Field. Hale, who had been a star in many westerns, was surprised to find a modern first-rate ballpark in the remote Big Bend country.

Sky King
Cowboy players look skyward for the high-arcing first pitch hurled by movie star Monte Hale. The first game of the two-game series was a dramatic debut for the new Cowboys squad. There were a total of 32 hits in the game, and at the end of eight innings the game was all tied up. The Gassers finally outhit the Cowboys, winning the game 16–14. In his first game in a Cowboys uniform, Red Swanson, a Louisiana collegiate star, went the distance to help the Cowboys win the second game against the Jal club 5–4.

COWBOY TALES Doyle Stout, pitcher

The big event in West Texas in 1955 was that the colossal film *Giant* was being filmed in Marfa, a mere 25 miles away. The movie, based on the King Ranch, had several major movie stars, including Elizabeth Taylor, Rock Hudson, and James Dean. There were many other great stars, but they don't fit into this short rendition. Dorothy Foley arranged for the Alpine Cowboys baseball team to visit the movie set. The Cowboys were given a brief tour of the famous house set and the well site and introduced to some of the actors. Although I have always been a great fan of Elizabeth Taylor, I guess I never realized how absolutely beautiful and stunning she was. It was not a long session with her, but I recall her looking at the small group of "Cowboys" and saying, "They don't look like cowboys to me. No hats or boots." Guess she didn't realize that the Alpine Cowboys was a baseball team, not actual horse-riding cowboys.

James Dean was a different animal. He looked different, talked slow and slovenly, with sort of glazed eyes, and he looked like he had just finished a week of rounding up the cattle or perhaps working his oil well. He asked me, "What do you guys do here for excitement?" I mentioned that one of my favorites was rabbit hunting on the plains of West Texas. I explained that you sit on the fender of my car and with a 35-inch baseball bat, we would chase the huge jackrabbits of that area and whack them. He thought that was the greatest thing he had ever heard of and asked if he could do it. He did, about two or three days later in his same clothes almost, a cowboy hat and boots, and yelling, cursing, and screaming the whole time. He swung a lot and didn't hit a lot but had a great time. I kept thinking he was going to fall off the fender and that I would run him down and then be infamous as the guy who ran over James Dean. He was most thankful and said it was the highlight of his time in Marfa.

Tragically, he killed himself in an automobile wreck some months later in California. I don't think that the rabbits have ever had a more convincing or perhaps crazy actor trying to knock their heads off. The rabbit hunt never made the press—such as it was in those days—but it was a wonderful experience and a great remembrance of the famous movie set and some of the stars. I sold my car for $500, since James Dean had used it for rabbit whacking.

Back to School

In June the Milwaukee Braves conducted their second annual baseball school at Kokernot Field. Described as the best baseball school setup in the nation, the three-day camp had attracted more than 85 boys, more than twice the attendance of the previous year, from all over Texas and New Mexico. Above: Principals and instructors of the 1955 class. Top row, left to right: Paul Waner (Braves scout and Hall of Famer), Billy South-worth (former Cardinal and Braves manager) , Herbert Kokernot, and Earle Halstead (Braves scout). Bottom row, left to right: Chuck Ellis, Tom Chandler, Moe Hedrick (Sul Ross baseball coach), and Pete Swain.

Country Boys

Art "Red" Swanson (this page) was an outstanding player from LSU. Scouts had rated him as the best pitcher in the neighboring state of Louisiana. The year before, he had won four games in the Louisiana State High School baseball tournament. Three of the games were no-hit, no-run affairs, and in two of the games, he did not allow a single batter to reach first base. Prior to joining the Cowboys he had been playing in Nova Scotia. Swanson fortified the young Cowboys pitching staff, which consisted of Don Pearson, Red Jones, Buddy Watts, and seasoned relief pitcher Chuck Ellis. After his 1955 season with the Cowboys, Swanson signed with the Pittsburgh Pirates, where he played for three years in the major leagues. First baseman Herbie Biederman (opposite page) and his brother Bob Biederman, who joined the Cowboys in 1957, had grown up on a farm outside of San Angelo, Texas, and they were both crazy about tractors. On road trips they would often ask the bus driver to stop at roadside farm equipment stores so that they could sit on the newest tractor models. Herbie Biederman was a big gun for the Cowboys when they played in the Grand Junction, Colorado, tournament. In the final game of the tournament, Biederman hit two singles, a double, and a two-run homer to help the Cowboys take the championship. By that point, the Sul Ross junior had really caught the attention of the big league scouts.

COWBOY TALES Leo Burkhalter, infielder

Tom Chandler was my high school coach at Adamson in Dallas. That's how I ended up at Alpine and Sul Ross. I was one of the high school guys who had the opportunity to continue my baseball career at Alpine. Other players from Dallas on the 1954 and 1955 Alpine Cowboy team were Howard Snodgrass, Tommy Bowers, R. L. Patterson, Red Jones, and Doyle Stout.

All the players looked forward to the road trips. Mr. Herbert would always have money for us when we boarded the bus. We always stayed in the best hotels and ate like kings. We could order anything we wanted and just had to sign the ticket. Mr. Herbert also included our wives on several trips to Chihuahua, Mexico, and Colorado, New Mexico, and Arizona.

Tidbits: When I first met Roy Lewis he told me his name was Sand Blower. I asked him why, and he said, "Every time I fart it blows sand." On one of our trips to Colorado, R. L. Patterson threw a French harp off the Royal Gorge Bridge. It played all the way down. Pete Swain broke his leg in Durango, Colorado. We were playing at the rodeo arena. Pete said he was the first baseball player to break a leg at a rodeo arena playing baseball. I usually climbed up into the luggage rack to sleep on long road trips. Chuck Ellis called it Leo's iron lung. Playing the Sinton Plymouth Oilers at Sinton, Texas, I was the lead-off hitter. They had an automatic home plate cleaner. The umpire stepped on a button behind home plate, and it blew air that cleaned the plate. It sounded like a fart. I stepped out of the box and told the ump that I didn't fart. He looked at me and just laughed. We played Fort Bliss in El Paso. We always visited Juárez the night before. We usually tanked up on Mexican food and cheap Mexican tequila. I was the lead-off hitter. I took a big swing and missed the ball. I swung so hard that I let a big stinking fart. The ump backed away from home plate, took off his mask, and said, "Did you shit in your pants?" I told him I didn't think so. He said, "If you feel that coming again, give me some warning so I can get the hell out of here."

I left Alpine and Sul Ross in January of 1956 after signing a professional baseball contract. I played one year of Class B for the Midland Indians. I went to spring training with the old Washington Senators minor leagues. After spring training they were sending me back to Class B. I had one child and another on the way, so I went back to college. I taught and coached for 35 years at Prosper and Spruce High School in Dallas, Texas.

Picture Day

The 1955 edition of the Alpine Cowboys, like that of the previous year, was largely composed of Sul Ross college players. Newcomers to the team included infielder Bob Frey, catcher George Martin, and pitcher Red Swanson. Returning veterans to the squad included pitcher Chuck Ellis, second baseman Roy Lewis, third baseman Howard Snodgrass, outfielders Pete Swain, Jim Hopkins, and Ray Van Cleef, utility player Leo Burkhalter, and first baseman Herbie Biederman. Pictured back row, left to right: Leo Burkhalter, Jim Hopkins, George Martin, Pete Swain, Red Jones, Buddy Watts, Don Pearson, Red Swanson, and Howard Snodgrass. Front row, left to right: R. L. Patterson, Ray Van Cleef, Roy Lewis, Tom Chandler, Herbert Kokernot, Chuck Ellis, Herbie Biederman, and Bob Frey.

Grand Award

Early in July the Cowboys entered the Grand Junction Invitational Tournament in Colorado. The Cowboys won the first game of the tournament against the Grand Junction Eagles 3–2, sending them to the elimination round, where they beat the powerful Casa Grande, Arizona, Cotton Kings 11–4. In that contest Herbie Bieder- man hit a triple and two singles for three RBIs, and Roy Lewis hit a triple in the seventh with the bases loaded. In the final game against the Cotton Kings, Biederman hit three singles, a double, and a two-run homer to help the Cowboys take the championship title. The trophy presentation was made the following week in Alpine. Pictured left to right: Herbert Kokernot, Tom Chandler, Dean Ritter (batboy), Herbie Biederman, George Martin, Roy Lewis, Ray Van Cleef, and Jay Foster (batboy).

COWBOY TALES Ray Van Cleef, outfielder

Three young Yankees, Ken Balmer, Tom Foster, and I, had just joined the team in San Antonio. Tom and I had just finished our season with Rutgers, where our team com- peted in the College World Series. Ken Balmer joined the team after attending Pennsylvania University. None of us had been west of the Mississippi River. We were young, naïve, and a bit jittery about being in the "wild" West Texas Davis Mountains.

After traveling through Marathon, as the road crept into the mountains, we were shocked to see three masked men in western attire pointing BIG six-guns at us. The driver, Bob Bilgrave, who had been on the team before, screeched to a halt, and the gunmen surrounded our car. I sat in the rear seat, and a giant of a guy jerked open the door, still pointing the gun, grabbed me buy my shirt, yanked me out of the car, and demanded that I give him my wallet and watch. Needless to say that occurred rather quickly. With that, the three robbers yelled, "Back to the horses," and climbed over a fence and disappeared over the hill.

After gaining some of our composure, we drove to the Holland Hotel, where Bob Bilgrave said we better report the robbery to the sheriff, who may be in the hotel coffee shop. Ken Balmer raced in and yelled to all of the ranchers hav- ing lunch that we had been robbed and they needed to get a posse! Gene Hendrix, the radio station owner, took us to the station and said he wanted to get the word out to the public. Ken Balmer sat facing the office door and was telling all of the details of our experience. Suddenly the office door burst open, and the three gunmen came in with their guns out. Ken jumped out of his chair and raised his hands toward the ceiling. With that, the gunmen pulled down their masks and said, "Welcome to Alpine." Wow! What a West Texas reception. The three gunmen were Wally Davis, Gus Bell, and Dan Blocker. Dan was the big guy who became famous as Hoss Cartwright in the *Bonanza* miniseries.

Los Vaqueros de Alpine

Fresh off their victory at the Grand Junction Invitational Tournament in Colorado, the Cowboys traveled to Mexico for a three-game series with the Chihuahua City all-star aggregation. The Chihuahua Invitational tournament was sponsored by the new governor of that state, Jesus Lozoya, who was on hand to greet the Cowboys and a large group of Alpine fans. Like the previous time the Cowboys had come to Chihuahua City, in 1947, the northern Mexican metropolis rolled out the red carpet for its Texan neighbors. Entertainment was provided in the evenings, and the Chihuahua residents proudly toured the Alpine contingent around town. In the opening game of the tourney, the newly appointed Mexican governor, making only his second public appearance since taking office, threw the first pitch to Mr. Herbert, as a military band with a drum and bugle corps played. A singing group serenaded the crowd while young girls in festive Mexican dresses handed out bouquets of flowers to the players' wives and girlfriends. The Cowboys won both games, but that was beside the point. Following the game, the Mexican governor presented Mr. Herbert with the trophy, given as much for winning the tournament as it was a gesture of friendship between the neighboring countries. Right: The Cowboys and their Alpine friends and loved ones in the grandstands at the Chihuahua tournament.

COWBOY TALES Art "Red" Swanson, pitcher

The summer of 1955 I spent with the Cowboys was one of the most enjoyable summers of my life, being around a manager like Tom Chandler and some great guys like Howard Snodgrass, Hoppy, Sandy, and, of course, my roomie, Ray Van Cleef. Ray and I attended Sul Ross that summer and stayed in the dorm together. I don't think I have ever been warmer, since we had no air-conditioning, but nevertheless it was great. The trips we took were always memorable, and always something happened to make it a great experience.

I remember our trip to Grand Junction for a tournament, riding in a station wagon, and listening to Herb Biederman identify each tractor we passed by the sound of the engine. I told him, "Herb, I've never seen a tractor." He replied, "And you probably never rode one either." Great times.

Leaving the team at the end of the year was tough, and Mr. Kokernot came to me on the day I left with Howard and Hoppy in Howard's car and asked me to transfer from LSU to Sul Ross. I thought about it, but the Pirates entered the picture, and I signed with them. Nothing, however, can ever take the place of those great times with some of the best guys around.

Home Improvements

In August the Cowboys concluded one of the most successful baseball seasons in their nine-year history, with a record of 23 wins and eight losses. After the last game of the season Mr. Herbert started on a major face-lift of Kokernot Field. The wooden fence around the ballpark was updated with a sturdy wall of native red stone that was emblazoned in several places around the perimeter with eight-foot versions of the O6 Ranch brand. The distinctive cattle brand, and the words "Kokernot Field" spelled out over the entrance, were the only graphic elements that Kokernot would allow on the walls. Catchers George Martin (opposite page) and R. L. Patterson (this page).

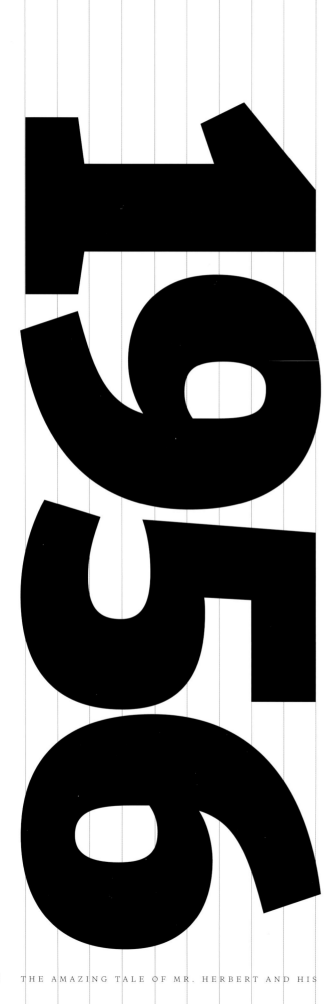

Fabulous Decade

The start of the 1956 baseball season marked the tenth year of the fabulous Alpine Cowboys baseball club, and Mr. Herbert had big plans for the anniversary year. During the off-season, he had a sturdy stone wall constructed around the park. The new wall was ten feet high, except for a 30-foot-high section that rose up in dead center field, and it had been pushed back an additional 30 feet, to a total distance of 430 feet from home plate. Ornamental ironwork lamps with intricate baseball designs were positioned at intervals on stone pillars around the wall, and arched gates spelling out the name of the ballpark had been added to the entrances. In addition to the exterior improvements, groundwork had been laid for the installation of a state-of-the-art lighting system.

Cubs, Orioles, and Jets

In early April the Chicago Cubs and the Baltimore Orioles rode into town for the annual major league exhibition game at Kokernot Field. More than 5,500 baseball fans from Texas and New Mexico crowded in and around the freshly updated ballpark to watch the highly anticipated spectacle. Once again, school was let out early and stores and business closed their doors by 1 p.m. so that employees and students could go to the big show. The Holland Hotel, where the two major league clubs were staying, was packed with gawkers and autograph seekers the morning after the teams had arrived for the annual big league exhibition game. At the game, the Chicago Cubs unleashed their power, rapping out 20 base hits and five home runs to rout the Orioles 16–4. Chuck Whitlock, writing in *The El Paso Times*, described this incident during the game: "An Air Force jet plane, apparently from Del Rio, 400 miles away, nearly stole the show. We make no charge that the pilot was buzzing the field—frankly we did not see the plane and we were told he was some 500 feet high. But hearing him after he passed over the field was enough for the crowd and the players. Russ Meyer ducked for a foxhole and so did umpire Stan Landes. People in the box seats ducked and everyone jumped as though stung. It relieved a lot of tension for a moment." Pictured: Mr. Herbert, center, hosts Jim Enright, sports editor of the *Chicago Herald-American*, and Clyde McCullough, Chicago Cubs catcher, who drove in six runs at the exhibition match, at a postgame barbecue at Kokernot's O6 Ranch.

Bombs Away

In June the Cowboys played a three-game series with the World Series semipro champions, the Wichita Bombers, for a special ten-year anniversary weekend event in Alpine. On the day of the game, hundreds of telegrams poured in, wishing the Cowboys luck and congratulating Mr. Herbert for his decade of service to the community and his championing of baseball in Texas. Lyndon B. Johnson, a U.S. Senator at the time, and Governor Allan Shivers both sent telegrams. The *Alpine Avalanche* ran a full-page ad congratulating the hometown team. The Cowboys whipped the Bombers 14–6, making their famous sponsor very proud on his anniversary day. Don Pressley (this page) was the winning pitcher, and Jackie Davis (opposite page) and Roy Lewis each went four-for-five.

Finest Ever

In late July Tom Chandler reported that several outstanding players had been added to the Cowboys' roster for the National Semipro Baseball Congress tournament in Wichita, including former Alpine pitcher and outfielder Jerry Mallett and E. C. Leslie, a versatile infielder from Lubbock. It was also announced, to much fanfare, that major leaguers Johnny Podres, the Brooklyn Dodgers hero who had pitched his team to the World Series championship the year before and who was currently serving in the Navy, Jack Sanford, stationed at Fort Bliss in El Paso, and Chicago Cubs catcher Clyde McCullough would join the team for the tournament. Bill Mohr of *The Wichita Beacon* described the excitement when Podres arrived at the tourney: "The Alpine batboy found Johnny both cordial and profitable. Youngsters bending over the rail next to the first base dugout and sneaking up the ramp behind the dugout slipped scorecards, baseballs and autograph books to the batboy who in turn got Johnny to sign them. 'I cleared a dollar thirty-five,' said the smiling youngster as he jingled the coins given him by the fans wanting Podres' autograph." In the first game the Cowboys romped on the March, California, AFB team 23–2, setting a new tournament record for the most runs scored in a single inning. The Cowboys scored 17 runs in the top of the fifth inning to force the game to an early halt under tournament rules. Podres pitched no-hit ball for four innings and got four safeties in five trips to the plate, including two doubles. Unfortunately, Podres had to return to the Navy after *The Sporting News* protested his pitching for Alpine. Although the Cowboys eventually finished third, they ended up with most of the all-tournament honors. A letter that appeared in *The Wichita Beacon* after the tournament praised the 1956 Alpine Cowboys as "the finest semipro baseball team to ever appear" in Wichita. Top row, left to right: John Kloza, James Thomas, Don Pressley, Buddy Watts, Jerry Mallett, Rick Herscher, Pete Swain, Jackie Davis, Toby Newton, and Herbie Biederman. Front row, left to right: Roy Lewis, Bob Quinn, Butch McCollum, Tom Chandler, Herbert Kokernot, Chuck Ellis, Howard Snodgrass, E. C. Leslie, and Ray Van Cleef. Batboys, left to right: Jay Foster and Mike Ellis.

COWBOY TALES E. C. Leslie, infielder

My experience with the Alpine Cowboys was only during the summer of 1956, when Mr. Kokernot and Tom Chandler were putting a team together to try to win the National Semipro Tournament. I had ended my professional playing days in the minor league system of the Pittsburgh Pirates and had begun a coaching career in Lubbock. Tom Chandler called and explained what they were trying to do and invited me to come to Alpine to play with them on weekends for about a month as they prepared for the State tournament and then the National tournament. The financial offer he made was so much better than I had ever received playing minor league ball. I could hardly believe it was true. But Mr. Kokernot was very faithful to the promises he made to those who played for him. I remember Mr. Kokernot as a very humble man who loved anyone who played ball for the Cowboys. He loved baseball and was willing to spend money promoting the Alpine Cowboys. By the time we reached the National tournament, almost all of his players had some level of professional baseball experience.

Crosstown Rivalry

In early July Kokernot Field became the site of the Northern Division tournament of the National Baseball Congress. The opening game for the Cowboys in the tournament was with the Alpine Internationals (pictured), a talented local Latino team that was sponsored by Mr. Herbert and also wore the O6 brand on their sleeves. Standouts for the Internationals were Gaga Llanez, Kachoo Valenzuela, and Vic Molinar. The Cowboys defeated the Internationals 16–3 in the first game of the double-elimination tournament and then beat the Abilene Onyx Refining club 12–0. The Internationals won their second game against the Petersburg All-stars 16–6 and then beat Abilene 7–2. That set them up in a championship finals match with their neighbor, the Alpine Cowboys. The winner of that game was to play the champion of the NBC Southern Division play-off, which was being held in Sinton, for the Texas State Championship title and a chance to go to the National Tournament in Wichita. In that game the Cowboys had no mercy on their Alpine brothers, beating up on them 21–5. Back row, left to right: Marcelo Alarcon, Unknown, Jaime Gonzales, Raul Molinar, Alvaro Gonzales, Victoriano Molinar, Felix "Gaga" Llanez, Vichy "Telo" Hernandez, and Pilar Llanez. Front row, left to right: Freddy Davis, Daniel Valenzuela, Ramon "Scotty" Escareno, Daniel Bustamante, Ramiro Jaime, and Roberto Hernandez.

COWBOY TALES Kachoo Valenzuela, shortstop

My name is Kachoo because the first thing I did when I was born was sneeze. I've played baseball for many, many years. I played shortstop for the Internationals, and I also helped with the Cowboys when they were semipro and in the Sophomore League. The Internationals were an all hispanic team, except occasionally during the summers when some university players played with us. Kokernot Field is one of the most beautiful fields I have ever seen. I would chase balls for the Cowboys, and I ran the manual score board at Kokernot Field. Mr. Herbert would give one dollar for home run balls collected and twenty-five cents for every foul ball over the fence. The Internationals traveled all over Texas and the Southwest. We were the most hated team because we would always win. We were a tight-knit group and really close with most of the Cowboys players. It was quite an experience. Alpine is such a good baseball town.

The Internationals practiced south of the tracks on a dirt field, but we got to play at Kokernot Field on the weekend. We'd turn flips just being on the grass! All the games were exciting, it would be hard to pick a favorite. Some Internationals players who came out for summer school ended up playing professionally. My most exciting memory was when I hit a home run at Kokernot Field in 1959. If you've ever hit a home run at Kokernot Field, you know you've hit a home run. I hit it 330 feet over left field. Later on they moved the plate back to make it regulation at 340 feet.

Tom Chandler was very strict when it came to baseball, but he sure knew the game. Gaga Llanez is an old-timer now. He's barely walking, but he's alive. He was one of the best pitchers the Internationals ever had. He also played for the Cowboys some. We had some really exciting games. One I can remember was actually against the Cowboys in a tournament. We played them real tough. It was back when Ray Van Cleef, Roy Lewis, Chuck Ellis, and Tom Chandler were playing. They didn't appreciate us hanging in with them—we weren't supposed to be *that* good.

Plymouth Rocked

In early August the Alpine Cowboys began a five-game series with their rivals, the Sinton Plymouth Oilers, for the Texas State Championship title at Sinton. In the first game, the Oilers jumped to a 9–0 lead and were coasting along until the Cowboys came alive in the seventh inning, coming to within one run of tying the game. Sinton ended up edging the Cowboys out 9–8. Sinton won the second game 5–3, but just when things weren't looking so good, the Cowboys bounced back with an 8–1 win, making it two games to one for Sinton in the best-three-out-of-five series. The Cowboys won the fourth game 6–5 behind the strong five-hit pitching of Toby Newton (this page), setting up a final game to determine the champion. In that game, Oiler pitcher Dewey Jacobs effectively shut down the Cowboys, giving the Sinton Oilers the Texas State Semipro Championship title. Both teams qualified for the National Baseball Congress Tourney in Wichita. Cowboy catcher John Klosa (opposite page).

Boys Town

Fresh off one of their most successful years to date, the Alpine Cowboys opened the 1957 season against the Roswell, New Mexico, Merchants, with a new roster of high school and collegiate talent. "This will probably be the youngest team the Cowboys have ever had," said manager Tom Chandler. Pictured: Batboys Mike Ellis (left) and Darryl Mueller kid around in the dugout with Mr. Herbert. He would pay the batboys for balls retrieved and give them travel money, just like the players.

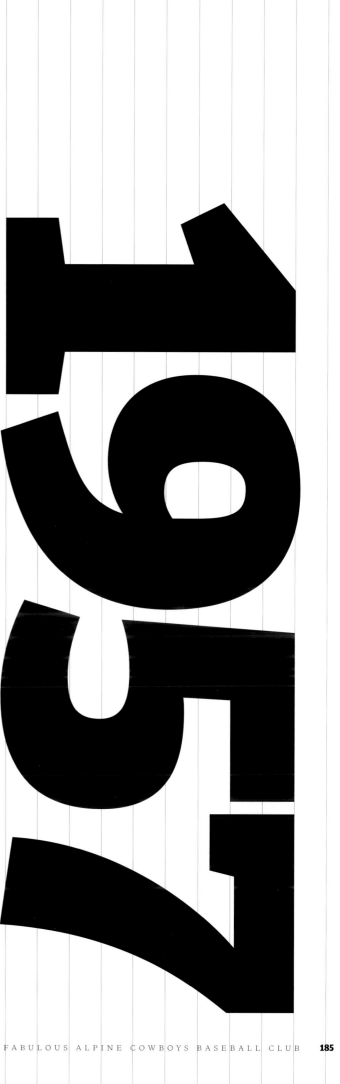

Wolff Gang

Debuting on the 1957 squad were left fielder Larry Click from SMU and right fielder Carl Warwick from TCU. Warwick later spent six years in the major leagues and became the first professional player to throw left and bat right. Other newcomers included third baseman Ron Dibelius from Marquette, catcher Pete Embry from The University of Texas, pitcher Jim Ward from Pasadena Junior College, and pitcher Jerry Wolff from SMU. The bespectacled Wolff, an all-around athlete from Webster Groves, Missouri, had been a standout at Southern Methodist University in Dallas before joining the Cowboys. He could also hit well for a pitcher, chalking up a .366 batting average at SMU, and he could run like the West Texas wind. In a tight game against Tarleton, he was on second when a high fly ball was hit into right field. Wolff tagged up and scored the winning run from second base. Soon to arrive, though, was one of the greatest players ever to wear a Cowboys uniform, a gangly 17-year-old pitching phenomenon named Gaylord Perry. Back row, left to right: Toby Newton, Larry Click, Pete Swain, Rick Herrscher, Gaylord Perry, Jim Ward, Bob Biederman, Ron Dibelius, Jerry Wolff, and Butch McCollum. Front row, left to right: Pete Embry, Ray Van Cleef, Tom Chandler, Herbert Kokernot, Chuck Ellis, Carl Warwick, and Roy Lewis. Darryl Mueller (batboy).

COWBOY TALES Carl Warwick, outfielder

I was invited to play after my sophomore year at TCU by Tom Chandler, who was my junior high school baseball coach in Dallas. This was Tom's first coaching job after graduating from Baylor in 1950. He went on to coach at Adamson High School in Dallas, and I played at Sunset High School in Dallas. Our friendship goes back a long way, and when I went to TCU, he was coaching at Texas A&M.

In 1957 I won the Southwest Conference title when I was at TCU, and Tom invited me to spend the summer in Alpine. It was one of the best summers I have ever spent playing baseball. In fact, during our first game at Kokernot Field, I hit a ball over the center-field wall. I did not know that it was the first one that had been hit over the center-field wall. After the game Mr. Herbert came to my locker and had the ball in his hand with a $50 bill and said, "Carl, this is the first ball over the center-field wall, and I want to buy it for my trophy case." I was shocked, as I had never seen many bills that big. Anyway, that ball was in the trophy case for years.

Dust Devils

In mid-June, left-hander Jerry Wolff (this page) struck out 21 batters and allowed only four hits and a walk, to wallop the Brownsville Charros 8–1. Toward the end of June, right-hander Gaylord Perry (opposite page), the sensational young pitcher from North Carolina, started in his very first game as an Alpine Cowboy against the powerful Brooke Army Medical Comets at Kokernot Field. Earlier in the year, Tom Chandler had received a tip from a scout in Georgia who told him of a wiry high school kid who showed promise. Perry, a junior at Williamston High School, stood 6 feet 4 inches tall and weighed 200 pounds. The eventual baseball legend and Hall of Famer came to Alpine in 1957 and spent only one summer developing his existing talent before heading to the majors and chalking up 314 wins during his 22-year career in the big leagues. In his debut as a Cowboy against the Comets, Perry worked six innings, striking out eight and allowing seven hits before reliever Toby Newton sealed the Cowboys' 10–7 victory. A dust storm blew threw and halted the game in the seventh inning for thirty minutes. It was a sign of things to come for Perry.

Baseball Nuts

At the end of June, the fourth annual Milwaukee Braves Baseball School was held at Kokernot Field. Once again big league legend Paul Waner and Brave's scout Earle W. Halstead provided experienced baseball instruction to young boys from all over the Southwest and gave them the opportunity to play in one of the finest equipped baseball facilities in the country. Pictured: Halstead and Waner sit in the shade as they observe the Cowboys' state-of-the-art ball machine pitching to a player in the batting cage. Also in June, Kokernot Field hosted the First National NAIA Baseball tournament, which the Sul Ross Lobos ended up winning. Eight colleges, their fans, and press from all over the nation made the trek to Alpine for the meet, and once again the little West Texas town became the focus of the baseball world. Carl Guys reported from the event: "We have the use of Doyle Stout's office for typing but are in the big fat middle of the Chamber of Commerce right now pecking Royally... Heard that Herbert will light this park for the '58 season and then there'll be a real big after supper session each night at the ballpark whenever his Cowboys or the Sul Ross Lobos play ball. We had occasion to visit with the man who does so much for baseball in these parts and if ya' didn't know he owned the place you'd never know it. If there were more Kokernots and less cocoanuts in the baseball biz the national pastime would be in a heck-uvva lot better hands."

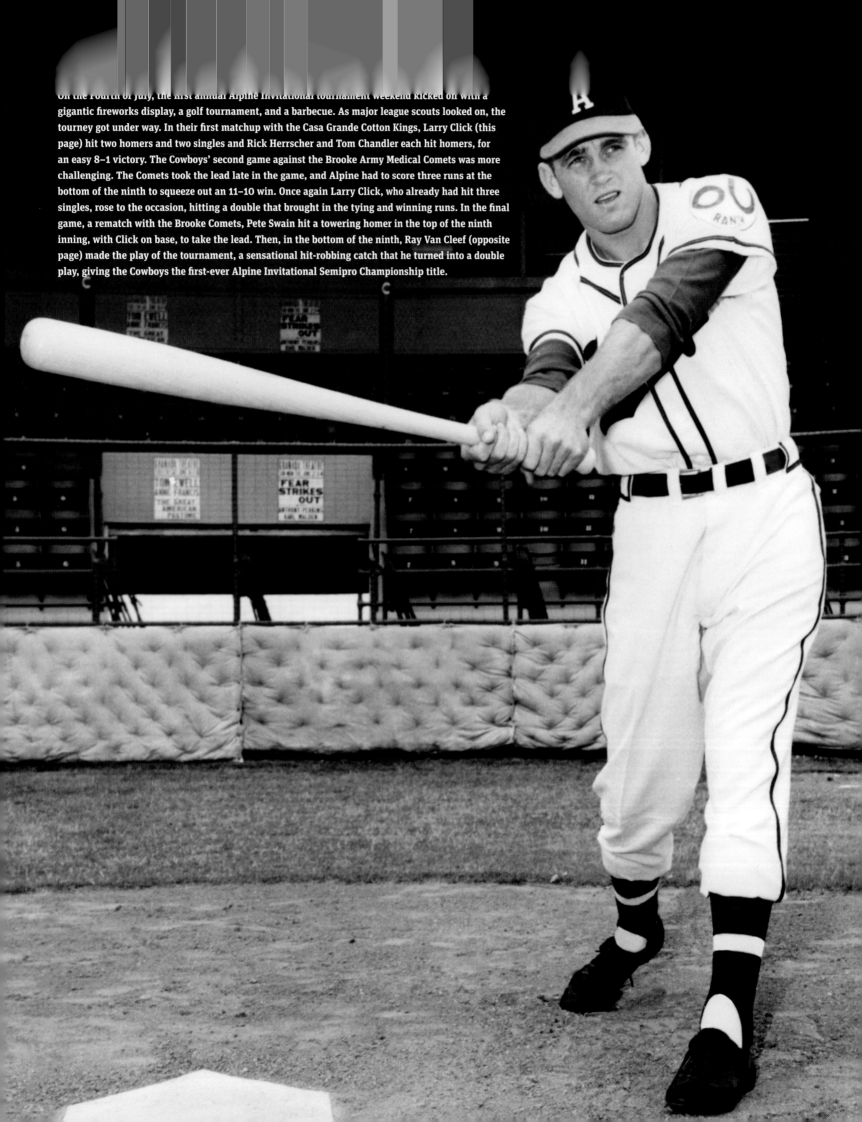

On the Fourth of July, the first annual Alpine Invitational tournament weekend kicked off with a gigantic fireworks display, a golf tournament, and a barbecue. As major league scouts looked on, the tourney got under way. In their first matchup with the Casa Grande Cotton Kings, Larry Click (this page) hit two homers and two singles and Rick Herrscher and Tom Chandler each hit homers, for an easy 8–1 victory. The Cowboys' second game against the Brooke Army Medical Comets was more challenging. The Comets took the lead late in the game, and Alpine had to score three runs at the bottom of the ninth to squeeze out an 11–10 win. Once again Larry Click, who already had hit three singles, rose to the occasion, hitting a double that brought in the tying and winning runs. In the final game, a rematch with the Brooke Comets, Pete Swain hit a towering homer in the top of the ninth inning, with Click on base, to take the lead. Then, in the bottom of the ninth, Ray Van Cleef (opposite page) made the play of the tournament, a sensational hit-robbing catch that he turned into a double play, giving the Cowboys the first-ever Alpine Invitational Semipro Championship title.

Trophy Girl

At the conclusion of the first
annual Alpine Invitational
tournament, trophies were
presented at Kokernot Field by
Linda Kay (left), the daughter
of Mr. and Mrs. Marvin Kay.
She had been chosen as "Miss
Alpine" in a beauty contest
prior to the big tournament,
and in addition to her trophy
girl duties, she also threw out
the ceremonial first ball to begin the tourney. The Cowboys,
as champions, received the
Alpine Chamber of Commerce
trophy, and the Brooke Comets
got the Holland Hotel trophy as
runners-up. Brooke shortstop
Matt Sczenzy received the
tournament award for most
valuable player. Jerry Wolff
(right) won best pitcher, Roy
Lewis was voted most popular
player, and Ray Van Cleef was
recognized for the most outstanding play of the game for
his spectacular game-winning
catch. Following spread, top, left
to right: Butch McCollum, Ron
Dibelius, Jim Ward, and Tom
Chandler. Bottom, left to right:
Rick Herrscher, Chuck Ellis,
Roy Lewis, and Toby Newton.

Staying Home

In August Mr. Herbert announced that the Cowboys would not be making their annual trip to Wichita, Kansas, for the National Semipro Baseball Congress tournament. Kokernot explained that several of his players had suffered injuries and the team was not prepared for national-level play. Instead, the Cowboys embarked on a six-game series at Kokernot Field. Pictured this spread: catcher Bob Beiderman, who was former Alpine Cowboys player Herbie Beiderman's younger brother.

Come and Get It!

At the end of August the Cowboys entered the Grand Junction tournament in Colorado. In a feisty game against Provo, Utah, midway through the tournament, the Cowboys showed that even though they had been plagued by injuries at the end of the season, they still had some fight left in them. A reporter for the local paper described this unruly scene: "With Alpine leading 12–8 going into the seventh frame the lid blew off. Provo pitcher Kent Peterson had been keeping his pitches precariously close since his appearance in the game in the sixth. Carl Warwick led off for the Cowboys and was hit by a pitched ball. Larry Click followed and went down swinging. Up stepped Pete Swain only to be forced into the dust by a Peterson shaver that hit his bat as he descended. Swain leaped to his feet, charged the mound, delivering several well-directed blows before the entire membership of both squads engulfed the mound and joined the fray." When the dust cleared the Cowboys had won 18–8. Alpine finished the tournament in second place, and the season was over. Back at home, Cowboys players serve it up at the Paisano Baptist Encampment. Pictured left to right: Roy Lewis, Toby Newton, Butch McCollum, Pete Swain, and Chuck Ellis. Above: Mr. Herbert with his grandchildren Chris and Elizabeth Lacy.

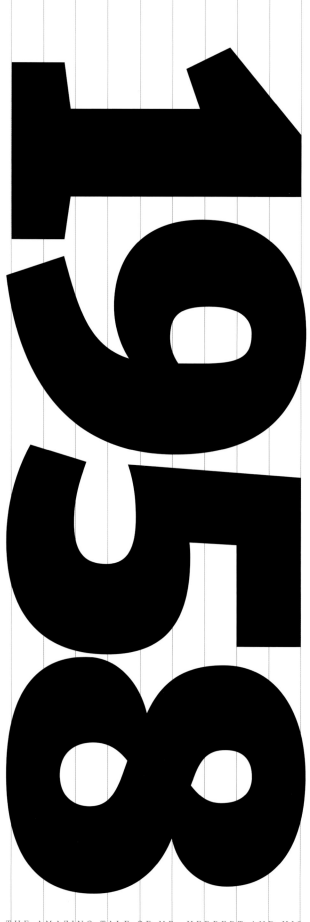

1958

Tower of Power

The Alpine Cowboys opened their 13th year of baseball under the lights at Kokernot Field. Mr. Herbert had been planning to add the lights for several years because many of the locals were unable to leave their jobs for afternoon games. During the off-season Mr. Herbert traveled to different ballparks across the country to find the finest lighting system available. When he returned to Alpine, he hired a contractor and told him, "I want lights better than Yankee Stadium's," and then shelled out $75,000 to have them installed. The sophisticated lighting system consisted of ten banks of lights mounted on 90-foot steel towers. The lights were positioned so that 100 watt-seconds of light were evenly distributed over every surface of the field, without hot spots or glare. Prior to the opening pitch of the inaugural night game with the Dyess Air Force Base Sonics, Mr. Herbert threw the switch, and the overflow crowd gasped and cheered as the field burst into the brilliance of 435,000 watts. Then they rose to their feet and gave Mr. Herbert a standing ovation for the dramatic light show they had just witnessed and in appreciation of his many years of baseball sponsorship.

The Cowboys were on and running under the new lights of Kokernot Field, sweeping the Dyess Air Force Base Sonics in all three games of their opening season series. Newcomer Joe Horlen, of Oklahoma State, pitched the Cowboys to a 9–0 win in the first contest, allowing only four hits, striking out seven batters, and hitting a double. New hitting talent for the Alpine squad showed their stuff. Left fielder Roy Osborne got three hits and two runs batted in, and veteran Alpine batboy Freddy Davis, proving that he wasn't just a boy who picks up bats anymore, got two hits, drove in two runs, and scored twice. In the second game in the series, Cowboy pitcher Roy Peterson, also from Oklahoma State, hurled the 13–5 win. Roy Osborne, Freddy Davis, first baseman Tommy Snow, third baseman Mickey Sullivan, and veteran center fielder Ray Van Cleef all hit doubles during the slugfest. Pitching ace Toby Newton hurled the Cowboys to a 5–2 victory in the third nightcap game, with Dyer giving up only two hits and striking out 12 batters. During the Saturday night game, longtime Big Bend pilot J. O. Casparis swooped low over Kokernot Field so that local photographer Charles Hunter could get a shot of the ballpark illuminated by the new lights. Casparis cut off the engine and glided low over the field so that the big crowd wouldn't be alarmed.

Short Timers

"One of the greatest seasons ever!" predicted manager Tom Chandler as he headed into his eighth year with the Alpine Cowboys. He had been manager of the team for six of those years. Tom lived and breathed Cowboys baseball. He and his wife, Willowdean, lived in a red-stone cottage that straddled the third-base line at Kokernot Field. He was well-liked and admired by everyone. Chandler had been a major influence on the many boys whom he had recruited to Alpine over the years. Mr. Herbert treated him like a son. At the end of the 1958 season, Chandler would leave the Cowboys to head up the Texas A&M baseball program, where he had a long and distinguished career.

Cashing In

Much of the raw talent that manager Tom Chandler and Mr. Herbert cultivated over the years eventually caught the attention of the big league teams. Over the Alpine Cowboys' 13 years of existence, the team had developed more top professionals than many of the professional farm clubs. Well-known major league stars who had once worn Alpine colors included Johnny Podres of the Dodgers, Lou Berberet of the Senators, Jack Sanford of the Phillies, Red Swanson of the Cardinals, Norm Cash of the White Sox and Detroit Tigers, Nobby Graves of Kansas City, and legendary Hall of Famer Gaylord Perry. Former Cowboys who played in the professional Texas League included Tommy Bowers, Jim Fiscalini, James Hopkins, Jerry Mallett, Bill McClarren, and Lloyd Jenny. Other named pro players were Ty Newton, Pete Swain, Tommy Snow, Boyd Linker, and Johnny Carruthers. Larry Isbell, Adrian Burke, and Yale Lary played baseball for the Cowboys but then played professional football. Larry Click, Rick Herrscher, Don Pearson, Red Jones, Herb Biederman, and Bob Biederman had all spent time in the pro farm team system. Kelton Russell, R. L. Patterson, Leo Burkhalter, and Howard Snodgrass signed with West Texas or New Mexico teams after leaving Alpine. Pictured left to right: Ray Van Cleef, who signed briefly with the Atlanta Braves and then returned to the Cowboys for the rest of his lengthy semipro career, Herbert Kokernot, and Norm Cash, who had a 17-year career in the major leagues.

COWBOY TALES Doyle Stout, pitcher

In 1954, Norm Cash asked me for a ride to Dallas so that he could spend the Christmas holidays with his girlfriend. On the way he said he wanted to smoke his Y-B cigar. I told him only if he wanted to go outside but not in my little two-seater coupe. He sat on the fender of my 1938 DeSoto smoking, I think his first cigar ever, while we glided down the desolate two-lane highways of that day and time toward Dallas. He got so sick that he fell off the fender but injured only his pride.

As we progressed toward Dallas, he said he knew exactly where his girlfriend lived. We arrived in Dallas about 2:30 a.m. and went directly to her house, he thought. The problem was it was not her house, and after about 20 houses the police came. Around 4 a.m. he finally found the girl's home. Obviously she was elated and the family overjoyed. Did he have the number? No! He just knew what the house looked like.

I tell this story because that was Norm Cash. He was not a detail man, not a Fulbright scholar, but everyone who knew him admired him.

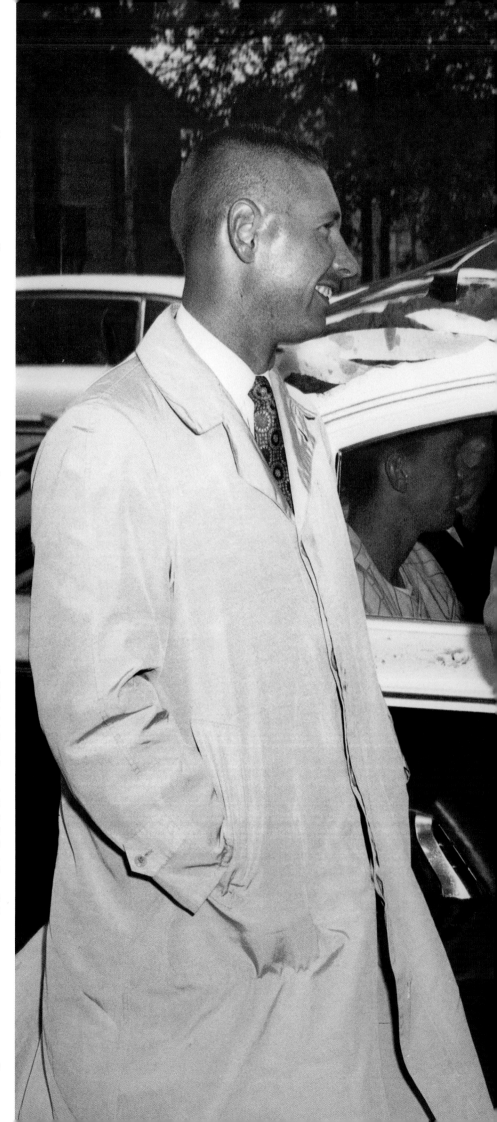

Snow Day

In August the Texas com-
missioner of the National
Baseball Congress, Jerry Feille,
approved Alpine and Kokernot
Field as the official site of
the 1958 NBC Texas Semipro
Championship tournament.
The winner of the tournament
would represent Texas at
the National tournament in
Wichita, Kansas. The Cowboys'
main rival in Texas, the Sinton
Plymouth Oilers, had won the
National title the year before.
This time the Cowboys, fresh
off of a spectacular regular
season, were out for blood. In
their first game of the tourney,
the Cowboys unleashed their
vengeance on the hapless Lubbock All-Stars. The score was
40–1 before the game was mercifully called off in the third
inning. In the second matchup,
the Cowboys walloped the El
Paso Merchants 14–1. Alpine's
Joe Horlen pitched a two-hitter,
and Tommy Snow (pictured)
hit a grand slam, leading the
way to an easy victory and the
Texas State Semipro title. Snow,
a University of Texas star, was
voted most valuable player of
the tournament. Now the Cowboys looked north to Wichita.

COWBOY TALES Tommy Snow, outfielder

Mr. Herbert installed the lights on Kokernot Field in 1958. Before our first game under the lights, Mr. Herbert came into the dugout and announced that the player who hit the first home run under the lights would get a one-hundred-dollar bill. The reaction was predictable. From the first batter even the obvious "singles" hitters were swinging from their heels. Batter after batter was swinging for the fences. I am certain the fans wondered what type of unorthodox team Tom had put together. The players would say a prayer, though silent, that the batter ahead of him would not be the one to do it. Some even cheered each time a batter failed, even if by striking out. Moans went out by a batter if he was given a bunt, take, or hit-and-run sign. As I recall, this went on for several games, even though we won most of them due to the weak opposition. Paranoia set in, and even Tom began to get worried about the team morale.

Finally, after several games, our third baseman, Gene Leek, who played for Arizona University, broke the drought and hit a home run. I don't think anyone shook his hand or even spoke to him for some time. After that several home runs were hit each game, even by the singles hitters in that high altitude. Things then got back to normal, and Gene, being a very nice guy, was eventually forgiven and accepted back into the group.

Last Dance

It was the beginning of the end, but the end was also a beginning for the Alpine Cowboys baseball club when they arrived in Wichita for the National Baseball Congress tournament. This would be their eighth appearance in the National semipro meet. The 1958 Cowboys (pictured), one of the strongest teams ever assembled, entered the tournament with a season record of 45 wins and five losses. They had just waltzed through the State championship tourney on home turf, and now they had a new swagger. When they arrived at Lawrence Stadium, Tom Chandler announced that the team would be strengthened by the addition of several pro players, including Red Sox farmhand Marlin Coughtry, former St. Louis Cardinal property Jim Hiland, and Dolph Regelsky and Glenn Plaster, who had been with the Yankees and Dodgers organizations respectively. Chandler also brought on pitcher Jack Shultea of Houston, who had been a standout against the Cowboys during the regular season. In the opening game of the tourney, the Cowboys routed the Westburg Long Islanders 13–1 and then narrowly defeated a team from Hampton, Virginia, 2–0 in the second contest. The Cowboys returned to their dominance, however, in the third game, destroying the previously unbeaten Bellingham, Washington, Bells 12–0. In the next game, Alpine continued their vengeful ways, trouncing the Cherokee, Oklahoma, Chiefs 12–0 for their fourth straight victory. "Never before has the field been so strong," commented *The Wichita Beacon*.

End of an Era

The Cowboys lost their fifth match of the tournament to the young but powerful Drain, Oregon, Black Sox 6–8 and then beat the Grand Rapids, Michigan, Sullivans 6–4, setting themselves up for a highly anticipated rematch against the Drain club for the National championship title. "Every one of their hitters is dangerous," quipped the manager of the Grand Rapids team, predicting that the Cowboys would win the title match. *The Wichita Eagle* ran a photo of Tommy Snow, Glen Plaster, and Dayton Todd holding bats, with the caption "Alpine's Murderer's Row." A riveted crowd of 2,500 fans poured into Lawrence Stadium and braved ominous clouds and lightning to witness the most exciting game of the series. The game was a tense seesaw affair until the top of the eighth inning, when Drain seemed to have the game in the bag, with a 7–4 advantage. But in the bottom of the inning, Tommy Snow stepped up and hit the top of the scoreboard with a three-run blast to tie the contest 7–7. The Black Sox came back with a run in the ninth and then held on for the championship, handing the Cowboys a second place finish. After the game, veteran Cowboys star Ray Van Cleef was chosen as the most popular player of the tournament. It was the Alpine Cowboys' last game ever as a semipro team and a dramatic and prophetic end to an amazing era. In December it was announced that the Cowboys would become a farm team of the Boston Red Sox, making Alpine, with a population of 5,261, the smallest town in the nation with a professional baseball team. Pictured left to right: Ray Van Cleef, Herbert Kokernot, and Tom Chandler at the end of the National tournament.

New Boys in Town

At the beginning of the 1959 season a Los Angeles Dodgers Convair jet landed at the Marfa-Alpine airport, and a brand-new Alpine Cowboys team and manager walked off the plane. The newcomers were greeted by 20 carloads of local baseball fans. Most of the arriving professional players had never stepped foot in Alpine—or the state of Texas, for that matter. At the end of the 1958 season, Mr. Herbert had completed negotiations for the Cowboys to enter the Class D Sophomore League as a farm team for the Boston Red Sox. The new pro team was now to be known by the unwieldy name the Big Bend–Davis Mountains Cowboys, in an attempt to draw fans from the entire Big Bend area. Top row, left to right: John Gould, Bob Statsky, Bill Jensen, Jerry Noone, Guido Grilli, Eddie Popowski (manager), Don Schwall, Gary Hess, Larry Vincent, Tim Carrol, and Ron Judson. Front row, left to right: Bill Moniak, Don Mack, Bill Lister, Brad Griffith, Ken Knutsen, and Knute Westergren. For more than a decade Mr. Herbert had fielded one of the nation's finest and most colorful semipro baseball clubs made up of college and high school players. Now his team would be composed of professional ballplayers, and they would all be the property of the Boston Red Sox. In March *The El Paso Times* wrote that Kokernot had reported the loss of a $7,140 diamond ring while he was dining at a restaurant in Juárez, Mexico. It was only his first major loss that year.

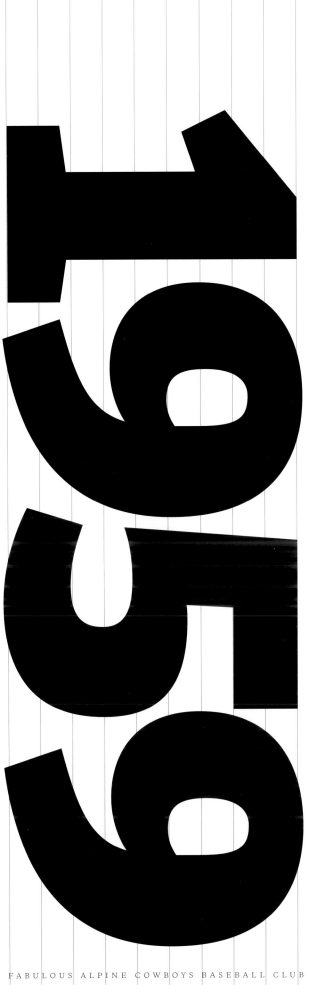

The Showman

In January, 27-year-old Gene Russell (second from right) took over as general manager of the new Big Bend–Davis Mountains Cowboys. A handsome city boy from Houston with a penchant for flashy tailored suits, Russell had come from a prominent baseball family. His father, Allen Russell, had been president of the Texas League's Austin Senators, and Gene had been business manager of the club for three years. Gene had inherited from his father a knack for staging circus-like promotions to increase attendance. Practically every night was a "special night," where qualifying fans could get into a game for free or for a discounted price. He featured family nights, ladies' nights, men's nights, student nights, date nights, camera nights, dance nights, singing nights, Big Bend Park nights, Marfa nights, Fort Stockton nights, Van Horn nights, and so on. He would give away hot dogs and peanuts and cheap souvenirs. On special occasions there would be elaborate fireworks displays, barbecues in the parking lot, and all kinds of contests. At one ball game, Russell staged a contest in which several Cowboys players tried to catch baseballs dropped from an airplane piloted by local daredevil and baseball nut J. O. Casparis. The Alpine fans responded well to Russell's promotional ways. Toward the end of the season the Cowboys games were breaking all attendance records for the league. By the end of June the Cowboys' total attendance numbers surpassed the 10,500 mark. True to Russell's style, the 10,522nd fan who entered Kokernot Field—that number was double the total population of Alpine—received two season tickets for the remainder of the season. Russell estimated that the Cowboys would draw 30,000 fans in 63 games their first year in the Sophomore League. "It's really fantastic when you can say that 10 percent of your city attends the games," he boasted. Pictured left to right: Ted Gray (06 Ranch foreman), Herbert Kokernot, Gene Russell (Cowboys general manager), and Dick Rogers (president of the First National Bank of Alpine).

COWBOY TALES Carol E. Sullivan, local fan

Ted Gray went to work for Mr. Herbert's father back in the 30s as a cowboy, and he continued to run the ranch for Mr. Herbert. Ted's brother, Junior, built the ballpark.

Ted didn't have much to say about the Alpine Cowboys baseball team. He wasn't a big fan. He went in to watch a game once, but he found it hard to watch because Mr. Herbert was passing out one-hundred-dollar bills to the players who made home runs and there were a lot of home runs that game. Ted, who was getting paid only forty dollars a month working out on the ranch, just couldn't make sense of all that money flying around. He never went to another game after that.

Yankees in Texas

The Boston Red Sox had sent down two of the most experienced baseball men in their organization to lead the new professional Big Bend–Davis Mountains Cowboys. Eddie "Pops" Popowski, 45, who was beginning his 22nd year in baseball, and his 17th year as a manager, was named field manager of the Cowboys. In his younger days, the colorful Popowski (this page) had been a member of the famous House of David touring baseball show, and he still liked to perform baseball tricks on the sidelines during games. The diminutive Popowski, 5 feet 5 inches tall and weighing in at 155 pounds, resided in Sayreville, New Jersey, and had never been to Texas. Prior to arriving in Alpine, he told the *Alpine Avalanche* that Boston Red Sox manager Pinky Higgins, a University of Texas graduate, had kept him informed about the "outstanding features of the Lone Star State." Fred McGuire, 59 (opposite page, right, with Pops), who had played for the New York Giants, was named full-time coach of the new Big Bend–Davis Mountains Cowboys team. The Cowboys had never had a fully dedicated, nonplaying coach before. McGuire lived in Newton Center, Massachusetts, with his family during the off-season.

All Hat No Cattle

The debut game of the Big Bend–Davis Mountains Cowboys was
with the San Angelo Pirates on April 27 at Kokernot Field. The
five-game series with the Pirates would launch the second year
of the fledgling Class D Sophomore League. The brand-new squad
of professional Cowboys arrived in Alpine just two days before
the season opener from Ocala, Florida, where they had been at
spring training. On the day of the big game, Alpine mayor W. E.
Lockhart issued a proclamation, calling for all businesses and
schools to close early so that workers and students could make
it to the Cowboys' professional debut. Tickets had sold briskly
before the opening day, and extra bleachers had been brought
in to handle the record attendance. Texas governor Price Daniel,
State Representative J. T. Rutherford, Red Sox president T. A.
Yawley, and Teofilo Borunda, the governor of Chihuahua, Mexico,
sent telegrams offering their congratulations. The president of
the Sophomore League, Grady Terry of Midland, threw the first
ceremonial pitch to Mr. Herbert at home plate to officially open
the 1959 Sophomore League season in front of an estimated 2,500
fans, almost half of Alpine's total population. Bill Winter introduced the players and managers of both teams, and the Reverend
R. E. Streetman gave the invocation. The Sul Ross band played
the Star-Spangled Banner as the American Legion Color Guard
raised the flag. It was time to play pro ball! Pictured: Umpires and
managers at the opening ceremonies. Alpine's manager and New
Jersey resident Eddie Popowski (second from right) wore his new
"Cowboys" getup to the gala event. San Angelo's manager Al
Bubiski (second from left) did not come dressed as a pirate.

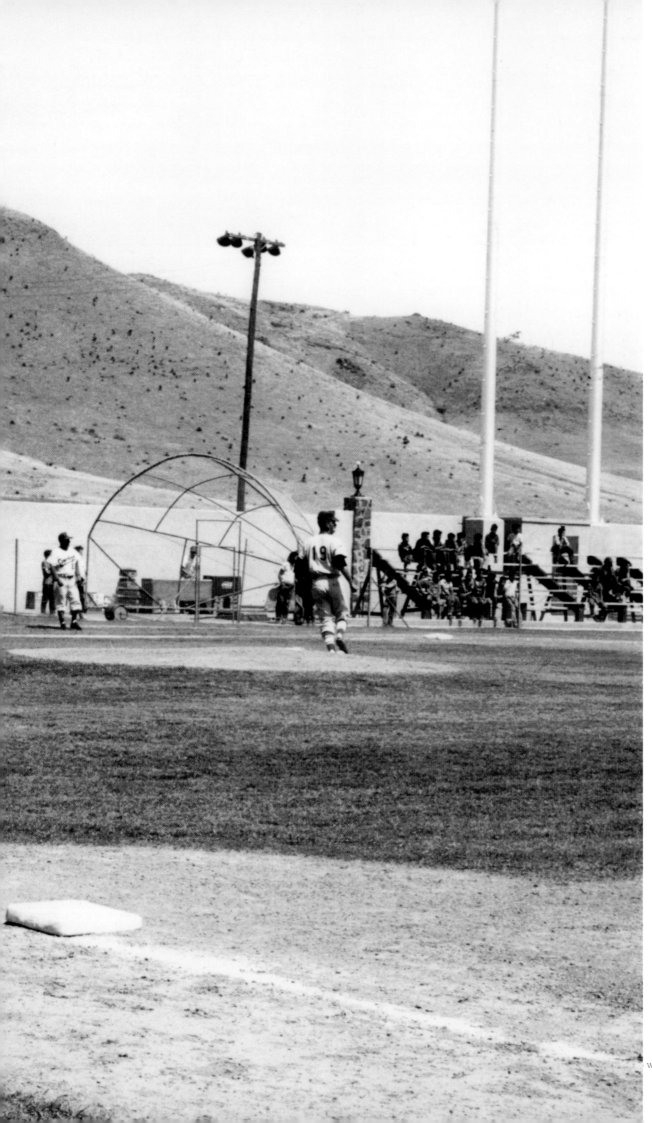

First Base

Despite the high winds blowing dust, with gusts up to 40 miles an hour, the first showing of the new professional edition of the Alpine Cowboys was a smashing success. The Cowboys defeated the San Angelo Pirates 18–1 in front of the hometown crowd, and as the *Fort Worth Star Telegram* put it, "Two of the happiest people after the game had to be Alpine manager Eddie Popowski (for 18 runs and a victory) and business manager Gene Russell (for attracting 2,500 fans)." The Cowboys jumped on the Pirates' starting pitcher Tommy Woods early, getting three runs in the first inning and six runs in the third. They got two more runs in the fifth and seven runs in the seventh off of the Pirates relief pitcher Charles Barrett. Cowboys catcher Tim Carrol hit a dramatic grand slam inside the park in the seventh inning, and pitcher Don Schwall went all the way for the win, giving up only five hits. The new Big Bend–Davis Mountains Cowboys were off and running. Following spread, top, left to right: Don Pressley, John Gould, Guido Grilli, and Jerry Noone. Bottom, left to right: Don Mack, Gary Hess, Hugo Papstein, and Brad Griffin.

Schwing!

The second annual Sophomore League All-Star game was played in early July at Odessa's American Legion Stadium. The contest matched up the best players in the South division of the league against the North division's finest. Five players from the Cowboys were selected for the South division team, including second baseman Charles Schilling, shortstop Jim Knerr, center fielder Bob Stotsky, pitcher Don Schwall, and right fielder Bill Moniak. The Cowboys' Eddie Popowski was given the honor of managing the South Stars team. In front of 2,213 fans, the South Stars pounded out a decisive 11–2 victory over the North. Don Schwall (this page) was the winning pitcher, and Charles Schilling (opposite page) hit a two-run homer and a double, drew two walks, hit a sacrifice, and drove in four runs for his contribution to the victory. By mid-July the Cowboys were leaving the rest of the league in their dust. Though only halfway through the regular season, the Cowboys had compiled a dominant record of 30 wins and six losses at Kokernot Field, for an .803 average. By the end of July the Cowboys had opened up a huge 20-game lead over Midland, the second-place team in the South division. The Cowboys led the league in team hitting and had five hitters over .300. Center fielder Bob Stotsky lead the league with a .357 batting average, followed by right fielder Bill Moniak at .351, shortstop Jim Knerr at .325, second baseman Charles Schilling at .319, and left fielder Larry Vincent at .316.

The Koker-Knutes

Toward the end of August the Cowboys easily clinched the Sophomore League championship with their regular season record. In a two-game series with the Roswell Pirates, the Cowboys' versatile utility man, Tom Roberts, played every position on the field, including one inning as pitcher, to help Alpine blast the Pirates 11–7. In the second contest against the Pirates, Roberts pitched the whole game to end the Cowboys' regular season play at Kokernot Field with a 5–3 win. In early September the Cowboys opened the play-offs with a 4–1 victory over the Cardinals in Hobbs, New Mexico, and then finished them off back in Alpine 11–0. The Cowboys' Larry Vincent got a two-run triple, and Bob Stotsky hit two homers. Gary Modrell shut out Hobbs on three hits to give the Cowboys two straight wins. That moved the Cowboys into a final battle for the Sophomore League championship title against the Carlsbad Potashers. In the first game of the two-out-of-three game series, Carlsbad surprised the Cowboys 10–3, but Alpine came back strong to win the second game 12–9. In the final game at Kokernot Field the Cowboys pulled out a 7–3 victory to win their first-ever Sophomore League Championship title. Tom Roberts, Ken Knutson (this page), and Knute Westergren (opposite page) all contributed home runs to the Cowboy's championship effort. Don Schwall, a 23-game winner for the season, was the winning pitcher. It was an ironic ending to the Cowboys' first full year in professional baseball.

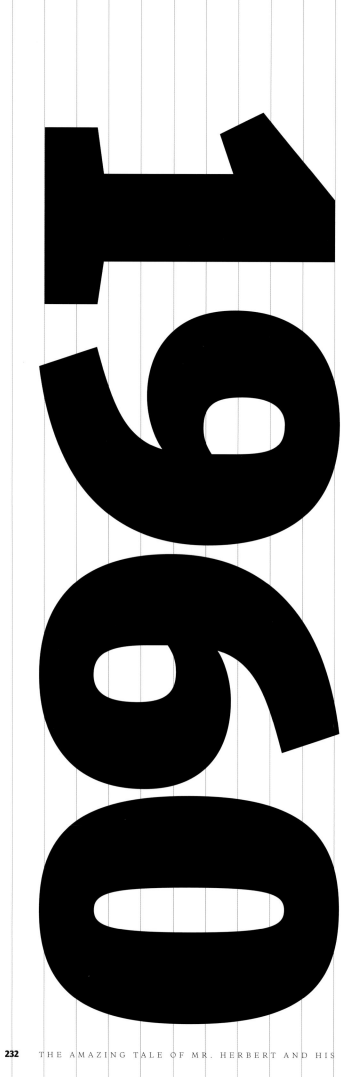

Tag Team

The Cowboys' first year as a professional team in 1959 had been a success—at least it seemed that way on the surface. Alpine completely dominated the competition during the jam-packed schedule and easily won the championship title at the end of the season. The 1960 season was another decent showing for the Cowboys, ending with a record of 76 wins and 52 losses. In the Sophomore League finals the Hobbs Pirates edged out Alpine, two games to one, to take the championship title. Back row, left to right: Don Sears, Bob Carlson, Tony Ankerson, Jerry Siegert, Larry Smoot, Ken Purcell, Jerry Brunelle, Bud Rowland, Darrell Farrar, Ed Coleman, Bub Blackford, and Larry Vincent. Front row, left to right: Ken Lawrence, Phil Scavo, Joe Cammarata, Dick Kinaman (Manager), Herbert Kokernot, Gene Russell , Ron Thompson, Mike (Moose) Imbriani, and Jim Fregosi.

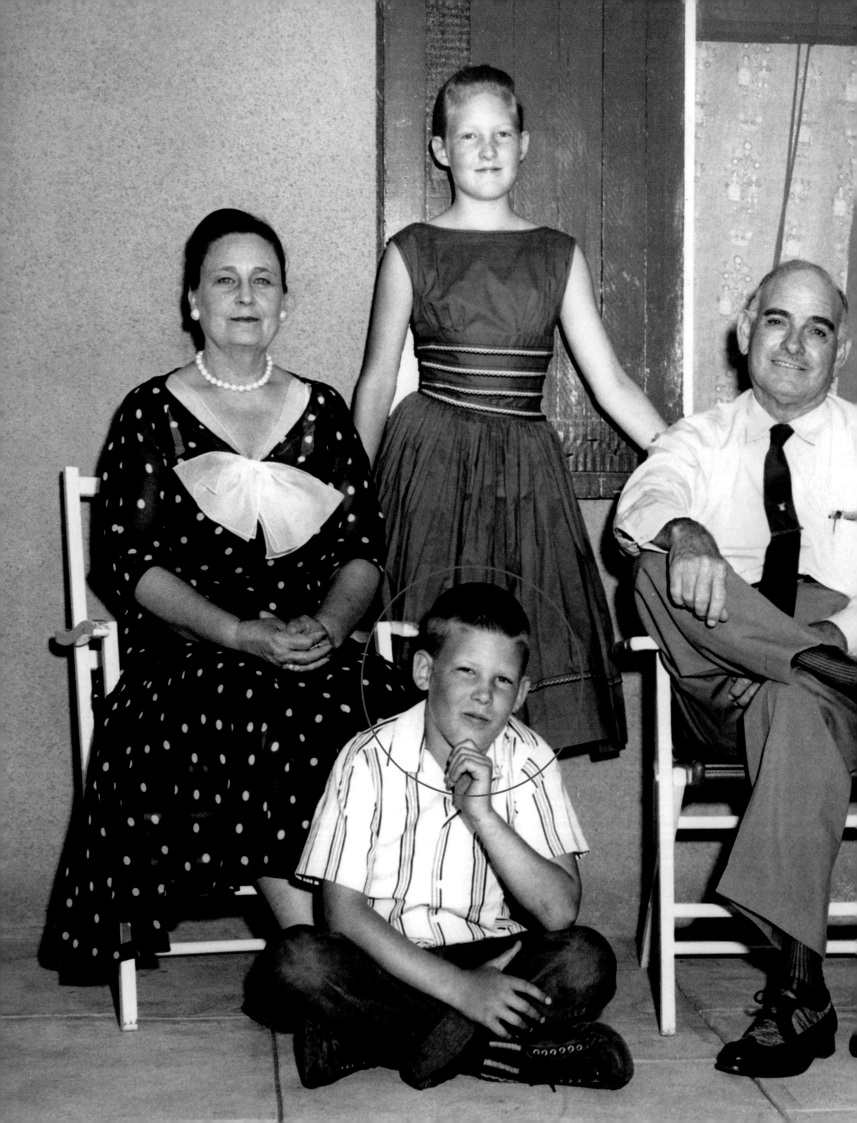

COWBOY TALES Chris Lacy, Kokernot's grandson

One of the main things I remember about going to Cowboys games with my grandfather was riding with him to Kokernot Field in his big Lincoln Continental. Oftentimes we'd pull right up to the third-base line and watch the games from his car, or he would park along the north side of the ballpark right on the first-base line. There was enough room on that side for about twenty cars to park side by side facing the field. Sometimes my sister and I would get out of the car and wander around the sidelines, or we'd go to the concession stand to get something to eat. Then when the game was over my grandfather would drive about a hundred miles an hour all the way back home. Man, that was fun.

That all changed when the team went professional in 1959. The only thing I know is that my grandfather didn't like it much. He didn't like the pro part because they tried to tell him what to do. It aggravated him that they were pulling players in and out all the time. It made it difficult to get a good team going. When the Red Sox pulled out in 1961, he didn't want to fool with it much. He told me that when they didn't have a Cowboys team anymore, he felt they did him a favor, because he was spending a lot of money. I don't believe that. He was just bitter. It really made him sad.

Meanwhile Back at the Ranch

General manager Gene Russell had kept the seats at Kokernot Field reasonably full of paying customers, but the farm team system had its limitations. The Class D Sophomore League was the lowest level proving ground for the major league Red Sox, so players were constantly rotated in and out of the Cowboys' roster over the course of a single season. When the 1960 season opened in Alpine, a fresh crop of young pro talent stepped onto Kokernot Field for the first time. The revolving-door practices of the minor league system made it difficult for the local Alpine fans to familiarize themselves with the team and to root for their favorite players. The loyalty and support of the semipro system, which had allowed players like Tom Chandler, Ray Van Cleef, Chuck Ellis, and Pete Swain to establish long and meaningful careers, disappeared when the Cowboys became a farm team for the Boston Red Sox. The team's previous owner and guardian angel, Herbert Kokernot, didn't like it much either, and he began to grow weary of the Red Sox management style. He loved the game of baseball, but he was becoming increasingly disenchanted with pro ball. He had always been in it for the fun of it, and now baseball had become an impersonal business. "These damn 'fessionals sell ballplayers back and forth like I sell my cattle," he griped. The Red Sox were issuing orders from Boston and making important decisions about the Cowboys without consulting Mr. Herbert. In a sense, the former "Sponsor of the Decade" had been delegated to mere fan status. He started to butt heads with the Red Sox brass, and he quit attending the Cowboys' games as regularly. "I think he liked baseball people even more than he liked the game," said his grandson, Chris Lacy, who took over the reins of the Kokernot 06 Ranch in 1987. Now Mr. Herbert was running out of baseball people to like. Pictured: The Kokernot family, left to right: Golda Rixon Kokernot (wife), Elizabeth Lacy, Chris Lacy, Herbert Kokernot, Ann Lacy, and Mary Ann Kokernot Lacy (daughter).

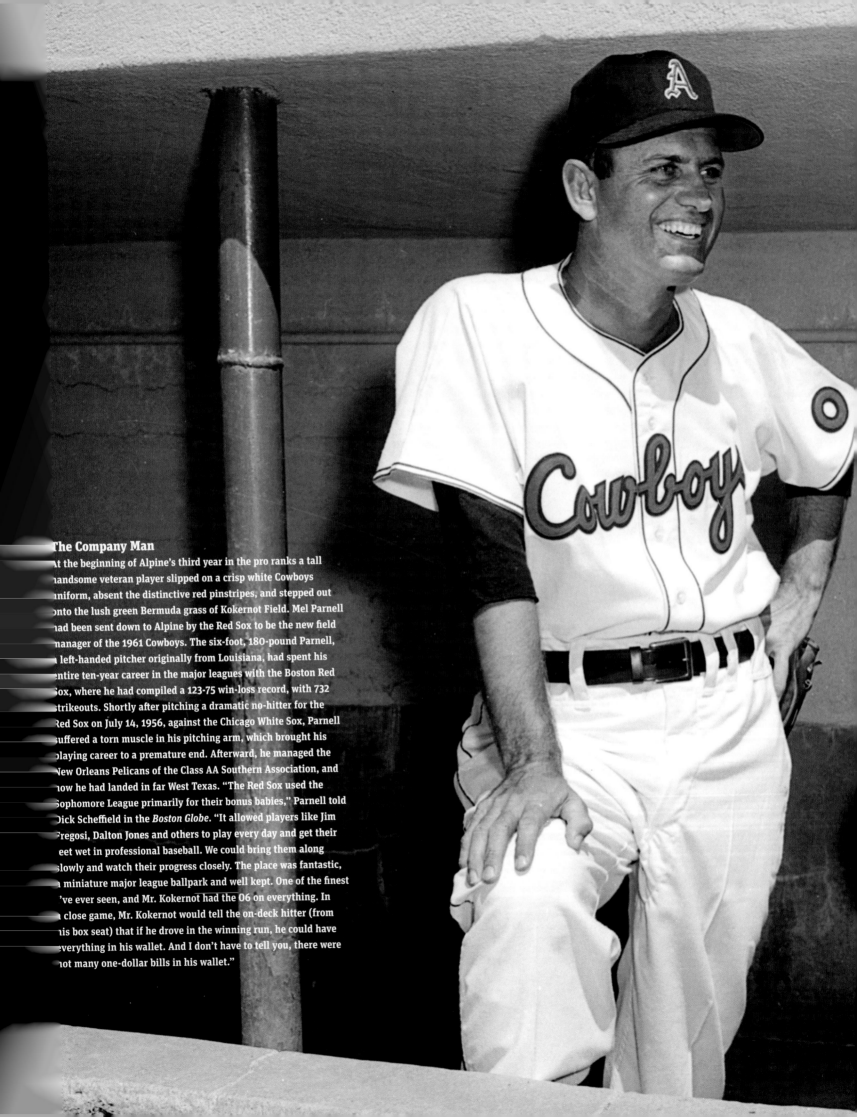

The Company Man

At the beginning of Alpine's third year in the pro ranks a tall handsome veteran player slipped on a crisp white Cowboys uniform, absent the distinctive red pinstripes, and stepped out onto the lush green Bermuda grass of Kokernot Field. Mel Parnell had been sent down to Alpine by the Red Sox to be the new field manager of the 1961 Cowboys. The six-foot, 180-pound Parnell, a left-handed pitcher originally from Louisiana, had spent his entire ten-year career in the major leagues with the Boston Red Sox, where he had compiled a 123-75 win-loss record, with 732 strikeouts. Shortly after pitching a dramatic no-hitter for the Red Sox on July 14, 1956, against the Chicago White Sox, Parnell suffered a torn muscle in his pitching arm, which brought his playing career to a premature end. Afterward, he managed the New Orleans Pelicans of the Class AA Southern Association, and now he had landed in far West Texas. "The Red Sox used the Sophomore League primarily for their bonus babies," Parnell told Dick Scheffield in the *Boston Globe*. "It allowed players like Jim Fregosi, Dalton Jones and others to play every day and get their feet wet in professional baseball. We could bring them along slowly and watch their progress closely. The place was fantastic, a miniature major league ballpark and well kept. One of the finest I've ever seen, and Mr. Kokernot had the 06 on everything. In a close game, Mr. Kokernot would tell the on-deck hitter (from his box seat) that if he drove in the winning run, he could have everything in his wallet. And I don't have to tell you, there were not many one-dollar bills in his wallet."

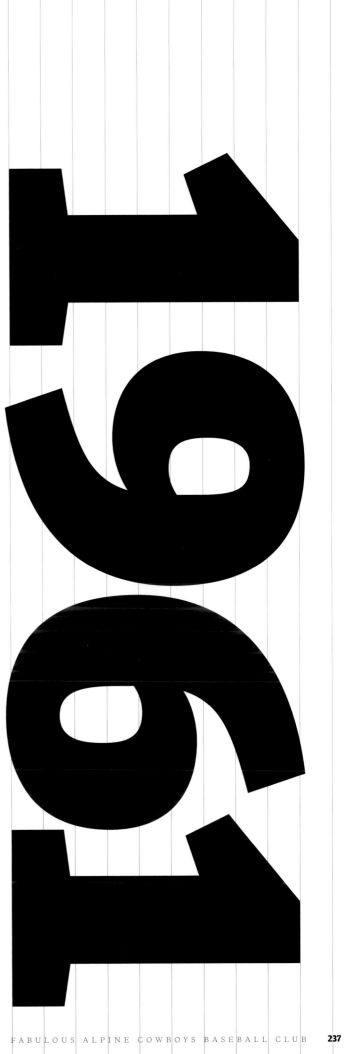

Last Pitch

Right-hander Harvey Casey on the mound (this page), the pristine walls of Kokernot Field behind him. When Mr. Herbert reluctantly agreed to let the Red Sox organization put a Class D Sophomore League franchise in his ballpark, he would not let them put advertising anywhere in the stadium, and he would not allow them to sell beer or liquor on the premises. Mr. Herbert had never needed the additional income generated by alcohol sales or the garish billboards that were commonplace fixtures on the fences of major and minor league ballparks all over the country. But now, only three years after he had made that deal with the Red Sox, Mr. Herbert could feel the walls crumbling down. His beautiful field of dreams was shattering. He was a West Texas rancher and financier with an independent streak and the means to do things his way, but now these "Yanks" up in Boston were telling him how to run his operation. The new players, like Harvey Casey, may or may not have known what was going on behind the idyllic walls of Kokernot Field—they were still having the time of their lives. They were young and healthy and living an American dream—and they got to play ball every day. They were a part of a baseball legend, and they were swinging for the fences. Following spread, top row, left to right: Walt Christiana, Pete Smith, Jim Moser, Dick Matern, Larry Wieck, and Burdette Morago. Middle row, left to right: Tommy Yost, Rocco Giordano, Don Sears, Stew McDonald, Doug Anderson, and John Harmon. Bottom row, left to right: James Shields, Bobby Guindon, Fred Hatter, Danny Cox, Jim Mitchell, and Ken Porter. Opposite page: Ron Thompson.

Leaving Home

Before the Cowboys reached the end of the 1961 regular schedule, the Red Sox organization decided to pull the team from Alpine. The Sophomore League was faltering badly, and relations between Kokernot and the Boston office had reached an all-time low. The professional baseball experiment in Texas and New Mexico had failed in a scant three years. For the first time since 1947, there would not be professional or semipro baseball at Kokernot Field. The new lineup of Cowboys players, many of whom had never been to Alpine or Texas before, would be shipped off to other farm teams, or maybe they would just quit baseball altogether. The dream was over. Fabulous Kokernot Field, home of the Cowboys, would not be their home any longer. Back row, left to right: James Moser, Burdette Morago, Darrell Massey, James Shields, Fredrick Hatter, Douglas Anderson, Ken Purcell, Dick Mattern, Bill Whalen, Walter Christiana, James Mitchell, Steve Cottrell, Jimmy Tyer, and Harvey Casey. Front row, left to right: Don Sears, John Harmon, John Morreale, Joe Cammarata, Mel Parnell (Manager), Herbert Kokernot, Jerry Brunelle (General Manager), Rocco Giordano, Ron Thompson, Richard Johnson, and Darrell Farrar.

COWBOY TALES Harvey Casey, pitcher

I played for the Alpine Cowboys in 1961, when it was part of the Red Sox organization. Mel Parnell was our manager. I was a right-handed pitcher and even "managed" the team for one week when Mel went to his grandmother's funeral in Louisiana. I had dinner one evening with Mel and Bobby Doerr, and because I was the oldest ballplayer on the team that year, at 23 years old, recently graduated from Fresno State, they asked me to take over for a week as manager. It was a lot of fun playing baseball in Alpine, and I played in the College World Series in 1959. The pay in the "pros" was not as much as I could get with my college degree, and because I already had a wife and two children, my future was in management and not in baseball. In 1961 the minimum major league salary was only $6,000 a year, and I could make more than that in business, so my family had to come first.

End of the Road

Former Brooke Army Medical player and major league star Don Newcombe once told *Boston Globe* correspondent Dick Sheffield this story about Mr. Herbert: "When he brought our club to Alpine in 1953, he gave us a bus to carry the team around. He told me, 'Don, you can drive this bus as far as you want and you still are going to be on my property.'" Now the last Alpine Cowboys players were getting on the bus to head out of town. The Sul Ross Lobos made Kokernot Field their home after that for several years, but in 1968 the baseball program was discontinued by the university's president. Mr. Herbert, who had provided scholarships to Sul Ross for so many boys over the years, was devastated and angry. He withdrew his support from the college and gave his beloved Kokernot Field to the high school, which didn't have the money to maintain it properly. Eventually the ballpark fell into disrepair. Weeds popped up in the infield and the stadium's iconic hand-painted wrought-iron baseballs began to fade. It broke Mr. Herbert's heart. Pictured: The 1961 Cowboys get ready to board the bus.

George Plunketo
940-382-7572

A Big Bend

In 1983 Sul Ross University decided to reinstate its baseball program and began fixing up the neglected ballpark. In 1984, on the opening day of the Lobos' season, Mr. Herbert once again tossed out the ceremonial first ball at the restored Kokernot Field. It was a bittersweet moment for the soft-spoken man who had done so much for the community of Alpine and for his beloved "Cowboys of Summer." It would be his last pitch at the West Texas field of dreams. Mr. Herbert died three years later and was buried at the O6 Ranch. There wouldn't be any professional baseball in Alpine for nearly 50 years, but then on May 17, 2009, the new Big Bend Cowboys of the Continental Baseball League took the field. The new pro team, owned by Frank Snyder and managed by JR Smith, will, at this writing, begin its second season this summer at Kokernot Field. The ballpark has been restored to its original glory, and the town of Alpine is buzzing with baseball excitement once again. In the 2009 season, the Big Bend Cowboys fielded the first Pakistan-born professional baseball player in the United States, and in 2010, the Cowboys signed Tiffany Brooks to a spring training contract, making her the first woman to join a professional baseball team this century. If he were alive today, Mr. Herbert would be very pleased with the modern version of the Cowboys, and he would still be in the stands handing out crisp hundreds for homers.

Doyle E. Stout Sr.

Most Valuable Player You have been my inspiration, Dad, for this book, and my life. I'm so glad you pulled me out of the pipe.

Christen Collier

Rookie of the Year Big high five for your hard work, enthusiasm, and design skills. You're a "Natural"! In "A League of Your Own"!

Julie Savasky

General Manager Thanks for backing me up on this and for your unwavering loyalty. As you know, there is no "I" in "TEAM."

Daniella Floeter, Anna Gardner, and Kelly Hanner

The Home Team I can always count on my Pentagram team to deliver. Thanks for hanging in there with me on this one, gang.

Lana McGilvray

Public Relations/Best Dressed Thanks for your amazing patience and for cheering me on every step of the way. I love you, PR girl.

Dave Hamrick, Bill Bishel, and Ellen McKie

Sponsors UT Press is my home-team advantage. I appreciate your support on this book and on all our previous projects.

Dana Frank

Pitching Coach I can't find the words to thank you, so could you please write them? We are always so grateful you're on our team.

Melleta Bell, Jerri Garza, Mike Howard, and B.J. Gallego

Team Archivists The Archives of the Big Bend at the Sul Ross University library is a true "Hall of Fame." Thanks for everything.

Chris Lacy

Owner Your grandfather has always been a part of my life. I'm so honored to be your friend and to tell the story of your legacy.

Willowdean Chandler and Charlie Davis

Team Historians There is no way that I could have pieced this story together without your wonderful obsessive scrapbooks.

Carol Lewis

The Groupie You have got to be the most knowledgeable person alive on the subject of the Alpine Cowboys. Thanks for sharing.

Cowboy Tales Contributors

Charlie Davis, Glenn Eaves, Bob Baumler, Ray Van Cleef, Ty Newton, Tommy Snow, Pete Swain, Doyle Stout, Willowdean Chandler, Red Jones, Leo Burkhalter, Art Swanson, E. C. Leslie, Kachoo Valenzuela, Carl Warwick, Carol E. Sullivan, Harvey Casey, and Chris Lacy.

Charles Hunter

Team Photographer Charles, I wish you were still around to see this book. I'm indebted to you, your talent, and your family.

David Wilkinson

Line Coach Thanks for throwing out the first pitch. Your generosity made it possible. I look forward to the big league follow-up.

Elizabeth Armstrong Parker

Trophy Girl This book has brought me full circle to the place where I was born. Having you as my mother is the greatest award.

Patrick, Nick, and Lucy Jane Stout

Bat Boys and Girl This story is a part of your lives now. I'm so happy to pass it down to you. You make me proud to be your father.

John and Ted Stout

Bull Pen We were never good at baseball when we were growing up, but you are the best. The World Champions of Brothers!